COUNTRY FURNITURE FOR THE HOME

The Kitchen

COUNTRY FURNITURE FOR THE HOME

The Kitchen

TIMELESS TRADITIONAL WOODWORKING PROJECTS

George Buchanan

CASSELL

Dedication

For Keasley and Elizabeth Welch

Acknowledgements

I would like to thank Alan Watson for the time he gave selecting
the wood from his large supply; Jennie Brech and Annemarie
Robinson for their help in choosing the furniture; and Nick and
Jane Parsons, whose dresser it is.
I am also grateful to George Sharpe and Richard Carr, who
designed the book; Bosch Tools, which are always ready with
helpful advice; and Rosie Anderson, Simon Tuite and Caroline
Hyams for their enthusiasm and skill along the way.

Disclaimer

While every care has been taken over the accuracy of the
information in this book, the author and Publisher cannot be held
responsible for any accidents related to products used by readers,
or to their workmanship.

A CASSELL BOOK

First published 1995 by Cassell
Wellington House, 125 Strand, London WC2R 0BB

Copyright © 1995 George Buchanan
Photography by Claude Hannaert

Distributed in the United States
by Sterling Publishing Co., Inc.
387 Park Avenue South, New York, NY 10016–8810

Distributed in Australia
by Capricorn Link (Australia) Pty Ltd
213 Carrington Road, Castle Hill, NSW 2154

British Library Cataloguing-in-Publication Data
A catalogue record for this book is available from the British Library

ISBN 0–304–34245–9
0–304–34243–2 (paperback)

Typeset by Litho Link Ltd, Welshpool, Powys, Wales
Printed and bound in Great Britain by Bath Press

CONTENTS

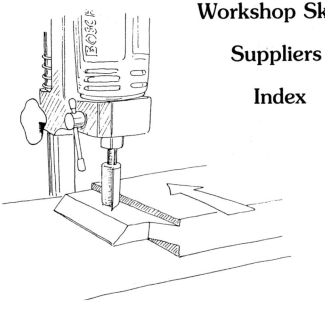

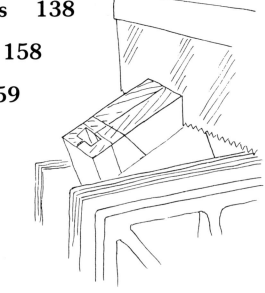

PREFACE

FOR MANY YEARS, I have enjoyed finding and repairing country furniture. Some of the furniture I have worked on has been English, some French, Dutch, German, Spanish, and some has come from Wales, Scotland and Ireland.

Country furniture is distinguished from furniture made in the large and efficient town workshops of the last three centuries by its ruggedness and simplicity. The designs of the country craftsmen reflect the popular fashions of the metropolitan cabinet-makers, but retain a simple charm which is unique. Even a set of country chairs will show individual differences. The execution is often a little crude, and the thicknesses and weights of the components are likely to be heavier than you would expect in a town-made piece.

I hope that by writing this book I will encourage people to make their own beautiful furniture. The pieces I describe do not require much skill to make, and I do not assume in my instructions that the reader will have a practical knowledge of jointing or a comprehensively equipped workshop.

Techniques for the necessary woodworking skills are described in detail, and I have drawn as many illustrations as I can to render the instructions clear and simple. Country carpenters were frequently not used to making furniture: much of their time would have been spent making gates, doors, rakes and wheelbarrows. They will have been familiar with using their tools, and as a beginner you too can expect to become familiar with handling your tools as your project progresses.

I used mainly hand tools to fashion these pieces and, although sometimes the work was physically quite hard, it was not technically very difficult.

Unlike the country carpenter of the past, who would have had to process much of his timber from rough planks, we can easily buy wood that is planed and sawn to size. If we do choose rough-sawn planks from a woodyard, then it is not hard to find a friendly carpenter who will saw and thickness them for us on his machines.

Hand-held, electric power tools make many of the more tedious tasks simple and quick. I use mainly Bosch power tools: jigsaw, router, planer, sander and drill. I also have a table-mounted circular saw. These tools are fairly expensive, but they liberate a craftsman from a lot of drudgery, and speed up production. If you do not count your time, then wood and tools are the only costs, and when you balance these costs against the value of the furniture you have made, not to mention the pleasure this hobby can give, the costs seem small.

The pieces of furniture chosen here are simple, beautiful and useful. The instructions provide an order of construction that is sensible and safe. You should find the processes I lead you through straightforward. Try not to work in a hurry; most of the pleasure in woodworking is in the activity, the delicious smell and feel of the wood as it is freshly cut, the beauty of the raw material and the excitement of working with it to create something new and special.

Finally, a word of advice: keep your tools sharp. You will not save time if you neglect your tools and you will not enjoy using them; also you are more likely to hurt yourself. I have included instructions here for sharpening edge tools, and most hardware stores will operate a saw sharpening service.

Good luck.

George Buchanan

SPANISH CHAIR

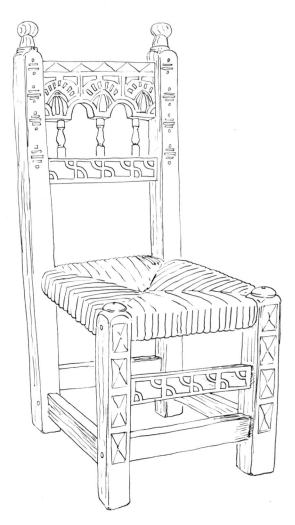

T HESE CHAIRS are copied from an old set of Spanish refectory
chairs. Their austere appearance is lightened by the arches in the
backrest and the relief carving on the front stretcher, the back and
the legs. The seats are rushed, but in the collection of original refectory chairs, some of the seats were plaited with string. For comfort,
the seat cavities were stuffed with padding. The finials on the top of
the chair legs are roughly turned. You will need only a simple lathe,
powered by an electric drill to do this.

The chair in the photograph (see following page 96) is made from
larch, and it was waxed three times with dark brown wax polish within days of being finished.

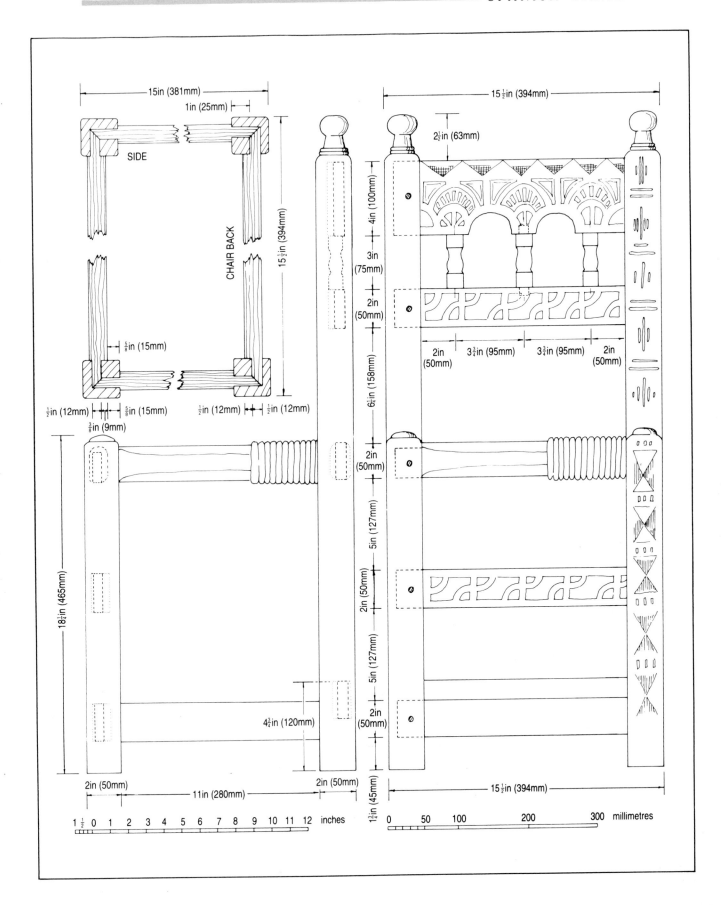

CONSTRUCTION

The convenient dimensions make it possible to keep the material cost of each chair very low. The instructions here relate to making a set of chairs, and include some suggestions for minimizing the time spent in marking out, and setting up power tools for repetitive work.

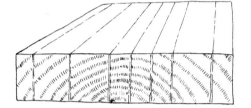

Select 2in (50mm) knot-free wood for the legs, rails and stretchers. If you are cutting all the components from a single slash-sawn board, first cut one or two ⅞in (22mm) strips from the edge for the seat rails. The wood at the edge of the plank is unlikely to be attractive, and is ideal for the seat rails which are hidden by the woven seating. Provided they are not weakened by large knots they will be perfectly satisfactory.

Next, cut the 2in (50mm) wide legs, and lastly saw the rails and back splats. Coming from the centre of the plank, these should be a rich colour with a close grain.

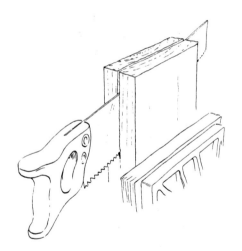

Then cut out the backrests. You will be able to cut two ⅞in (22mm) thick backrests from a 2in (50mm) thick plank , but because they are so wide, (4in/100mm), sawing them to thickness with a handsaw will be laborious. So, once you have cut out the block from which the backrests will be taken, cut around the edges of the plank with a circular saw, and use a handsaw to slice through the remaining wood. For advice on using a circular saw see page 142. Plane all the components to their finished dimensions. One pair of adjacent faces on each pair of legs should be planed square, but none of the other planing needs to be precise.

When you have reached this stage, lay out all the components and check that there are enough of each. It is extremely frustrating to discover when you have almost finished assembling a set of chairs that you are one rail or stretcher short. Making good the deficiency takes a disproportionate amount of time.

Plane the rails and stretchers smooth. They should all be about the same width and thickness. If you are making more than one chair at a time, the pile of rails and stretchers will be too big to sensibly allocate them to particular joints. So find the narrowest one of all, which will need the shortest mortice, and when you are making the cardboard template, measure and cut the mortices in the template to that length; deeper tenons can be easily shaved to fit.

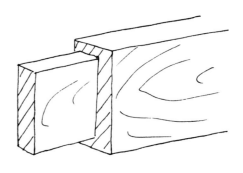

Cardboard template

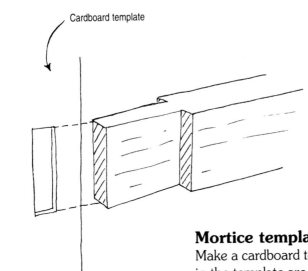

Mortice template

Make a cardboard template as illustrated on page 10. The slots in the template are the mortices, and the template is reversible so that the same template can be used for marking the joints on all four legs.

Making the legs

Saw the legs to length. The sawcut at the bottom of the leg should be square and accurate because it is the reference point for the template. Leave about $\frac{1}{2}$ in (12mm) waste at the top of the leg for trimming.

Turning the back leg finials

Mark the shoulder-line for the finials, as illustrated, and then make the simple wooden tool which marks the major shapes. Panel pins driven well into the tool and snipped off $\frac{1}{8}$ in (4mm) clear of its face will scratch the marks directly onto the revolving leg.

Take each leg in turn. At either end, mark the centrepoint, and indent it with a centrepunch or large nail. Before turning the first leg, remove the sharp corners with a chisel.

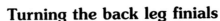

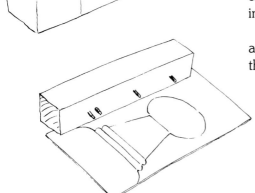

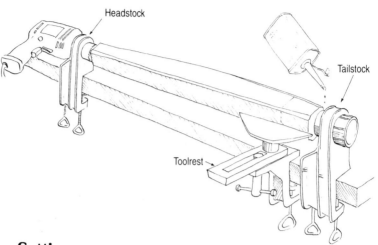

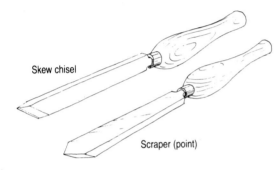

Skew chisel

Scraper (point)

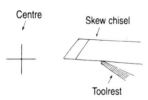

Centre

Skew chisel

Toolrest

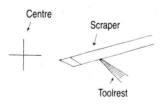

Centre

Scraper

Toolrest

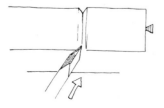

Setting up

Place the leg between the centres of the lathe, and adjust the toolrest so that it is parallel to and level with the axis of the leg. Lubricate the tailstock end with a drop of oil.

There is a benefit in turning these finials crudely, using scraper tools. Scrapers are very easy to use and control, and are quick and easy to sharpen (see page 147). For most woodturning, the disadvantage of using scrapers is that they tear the wood grain, particularly where the timber displays prominent growth rings. But these chairs are rather crudely constructed, and although the rough and splintered finials left by the scraper may be a little embarrassing at first, with constant use (as handholds when drawing out the chair), they will become smooth and silky, with a rich and attractive colour. Perfectly turned finials will need a lot rougher treatment before they appear as beautiful.

You will need two tools for turning the finials on the chair backs: a small skew chisel for making the initial incisions at the shoulder and for shaping the twin beads at the base of the finial, and a diamond point scraper for shaping the ball at the top of the finial and the sweep leading to it.

The sequence of illustrations shows the order in which the finials are turned. Hold the turning tools with both hands. The skew chisel is used upside down, so that only the very point touches the work, and the scraper should be kept so that the point is a little below the axis of the leg, where it is a little less likely to chatter and chip out large chunks of wood.

First turning

Start the turning with the skew chisel, and use it to incise a shoulder-line 3in (75mm) from the end of the leg. Now use the diamond point tool to reduce the top of the leg to a cylinder.

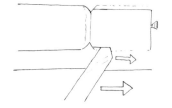

This can be achieved in three or four passes, cutting away from the shoulder. Stop the lathe and check that you have removed all the flat surfaces from the top of the leg.

Marking out

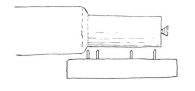

Set the speed to slow, hold the marking tool against the rotating cylinder, and press it there while the nail ends scratch their marks for the finial.

Increase the speed of the lathe again. Use the inverted skew chisel to define the cut above the beads and the cuts above and below the ball at the top of the leg.

Now use the diamond point tool to cut the sweep from the bead to the ball, then use it again to shape the ball, always working from greater to smaller diameters.

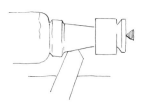 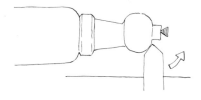

Shaping

When you are happy with the shapes so far, use the very point of the skew chisel to define the beads. Then use it again to sneak around the top of the ball, to weaken the short stub of wood connecting the leg to the tailstock centre. Stop the lathe, and inspect your work. It will look a lot rougher than expected, but if you are happy with the shapes you have cut, prepare to sand the finial.

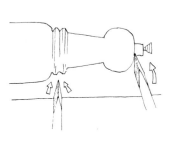

Select some unused 90 grit sandpaper and, with the paper face down on the bench, reinforce the back with several strips of masking tape. Cut off a thin strip, about 1in (25mm) wide, arrange a vacuum cleaner to collect the dust, or put on a face mask, and start the lathe. Run the lathe at high speed, hold the ends of the strip, and pull the strip against the rotating work.

Concentrate on smoothing the shoulder, the ball and the sweep that supports it. Then use a 150 grit strip in the same manner to sand the beads and the rest of the finial.

Repeat this for all the other back legs, and then sort them into pairs with similar finials.

Turning the front legs

Punch the centres of the ends of the front legs, then place the first leg between the lathe centres. Incise the shoulder as described above, using the inverted skew chisel, then use the diamond point to produce a short cylinder. Continue using the same tool, sweeping it across the end of the cylinder, until you have shaped the domed top. Now use the skew to undercut the dome at the shoulder, and to weaken the narrow stub linking the leg to the tailstock.

When all of the legs have been turned, take them one at a time, and remove the stubs from the top with a tenon saw. Smooth the tops of the legs, first with a sharp chisel, and then with some 150 grit paper pressed against a foam pad.

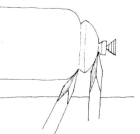

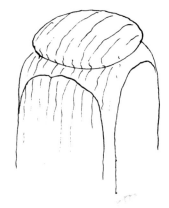

Morticing the legs

All the mortice and tenon joints in these chairs are ½in (12mm) wide and 1½in (38mm) deep. You will need the router box described on page 15 and a ½in (12mm) straight two-flute cutter to fit in the router.

Collect the legs into groups, with two back legs and two front legs per group. Now check and mark the face edge and face side of each leg, and use the cardboard joint template to pencil in the outline of each mortice. Remember that you are making a square framework, so the template will have to be flipped for the opposite legs. If you mark all the legs of one chair before moving to the next pile of legs, you are unlikely to make a mistake.

The plans and illustration show the offsets for the sides of the mortice. The corner from which the measurements are taken is the inside corner of each leg. It is quite likely that the faces of the rails and stretchers will

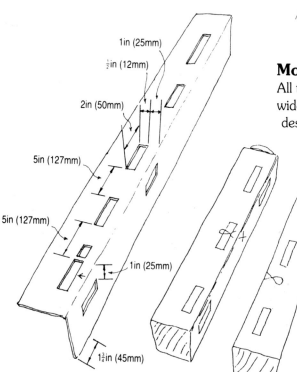

1in (25mm)
½in (12mm)
2in (50mm)
5in (127mm)
5in (127mm)
1in (25mm)
1¾in (45mm)

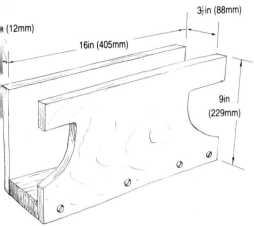

appear to be set back by differing amounts, because of the variations in leg thickness. This subtle evidence of crude construction is the sort of authenic detail you want to keep.

Clamp the first leg in the router box, with its face side pressed against the side of the box closest to you. Adjust the router fence so that the cutter is immediately over the marks of the mortice. After zeroing the cutter on the surface of the leg, set the depth stop to 1½in (38mm). Before beginning to plunge out the first row of mortices, support the leg by clamping a long batten to the side of the router box, underneath the leg. This will make it easier to reposition and change the workpiece.

Plunge out all the mortices in all the legs, keeping inside the endlines drawn from the template. When you have done this, knock the dust from each mortice and check that their sides and bottoms are clean and level. Then put the legs to one side and cut the tenons.

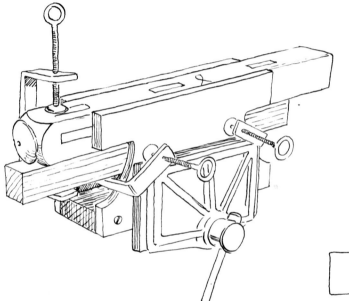

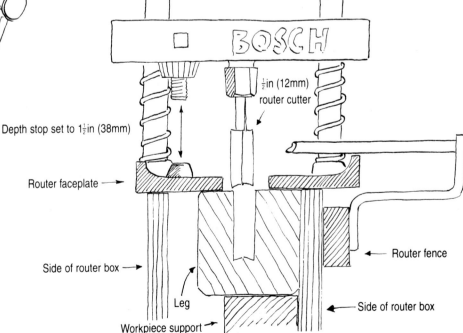

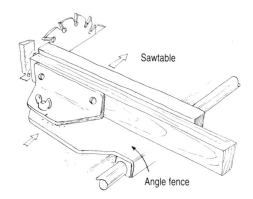

Sawtable

Angle fence

Cutting the tenons

Inspect the heap of assorted rails and stretchers, and sort them into two piles. Into one, put all the rails and stretchers that stretch between the back legs and between the front legs. You will need five per chair, all the same length. The other pile should consist of the shorter side stretchers and rails (four per chair). While you are sorting them, remember to choose the less attractive woods for the seat stretchers, and the better quality strips for the front-facing carved rails.

To cut the two piles to their respective lengths, set up the angle-cutting fence of the circular saw bench to 90°, and take a shaving from the end of each piece, to leave the end perfectly square.

Cutting the stretchers

Cut the stretchers exactly to length. Clamp a stop on the angle fence 14½in (370mm) from the sawblade, then take one stretcher from the first pile, hold the freshly sawn end against the stop and saw off the waste from the other end. When all the first pile, including the wide backrests, have been trimmed, move the stop ½in (12mm) towards the blade and trim the second pile (side rails) to length.

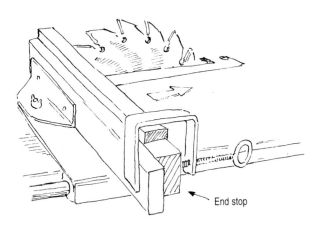

End stop

Now cut the faces of the tenons. Adjust the height of the circular sawblade so that it makes a 1½in (38mm) deep cut, and set the parallel fence to ¾in (20mm). Make and use the home-made tenon support jig to hold the rails vertically against the parallel fence as you push them across the sawblade. The first setting will cut the back faces of the tenons.

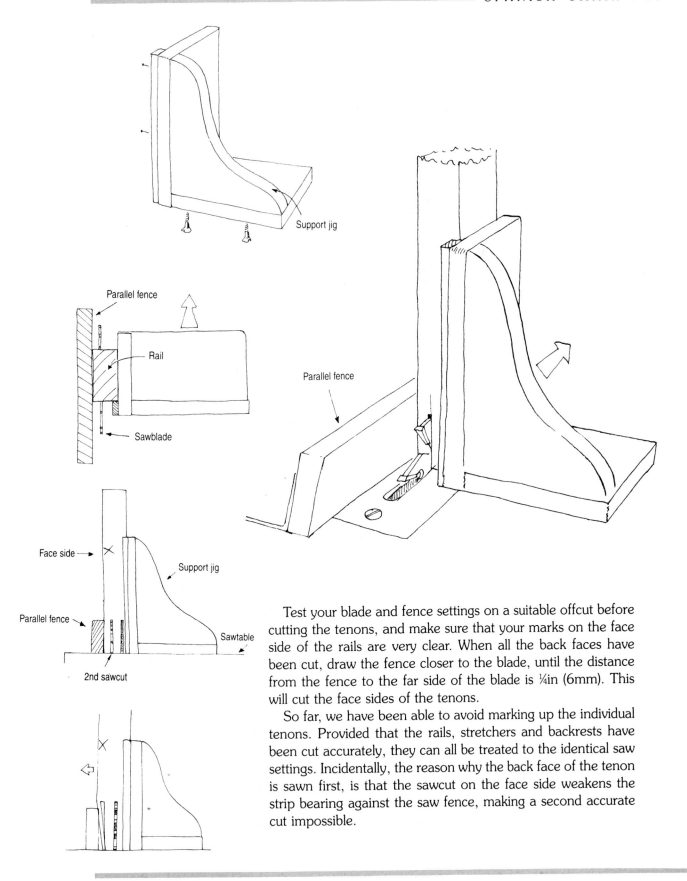

Support jig

Parallel fence

Rail

Sawblade

Parallel fence

Face side

Support jig

Parallel fence

Sawtable

2nd sawcut

Test your blade and fence settings on a suitable offcut before cutting the tenons, and make sure that your marks on the face side of the rails are very clear. When all the back faces have been cut, draw the fence closer to the blade, until the distance from the fence to the far side of the blade is ¼in (6mm). This will cut the face sides of the tenons.

So far, we have been able to avoid marking up the individual tenons. Provided that the rails, stretchers and backrests have been cut accurately, they can all be treated to the identical saw settings. Incidentally, the reason why the back face of the tenon is sawn first, is that the sawcut on the face side weakens the strip bearing against the saw fence, making a second accurate cut impossible.

Cutting the shoulders

Lower the blade until only ¼in (6mm) of blade is showing. Set the parallel fence so that the distance from the farthest edge of the sawblade to the parallel fence is 1½in (38mm), which is the length of the tenons, and cut the shoulders on the face sides of the tenons. The waste wood from the cheek of the tenon should fall away. If it does not, you should alter the setting until it does. If the sawblade is set too high it will weaken the tenon, so you must check for this and lower the blade if necessary.

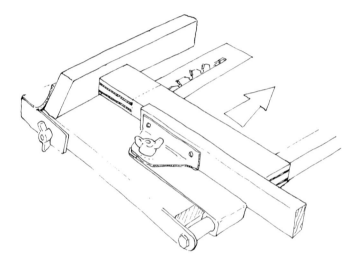

When all the face sides are cut, readjust the height of the blade so that it just removes the waste from the back. You must be careful when cutting the back shoulders, as the rails and backs are of differing thicknesses; it is worth continually checking the tenons against the blade before cutting.

Inspect each tenon and trim the shoulder cuts with a chisel where required. Do not go to the trouble of fitting the chairs together at this stage, but arrange separate piles for each chair. Separate and bind together the short side rails and stretchers in each pile.

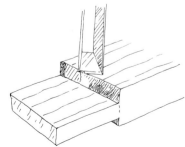

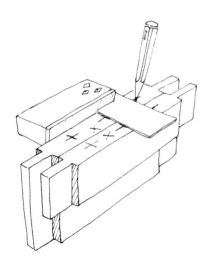

Backrest spindle holes

Select the backrest and the narrow rail that fits beneath it from the first pile. Align them in the vice, face sides together, and mark the positions for the three holes for the pillars, squaring across the two edges with a set-square and pencil, as illustrated. Do the same for the other chairs.

Drilling

Fit a ⅜in (9mm) brad-point drill in the pillar drill, and arrange a fence so that when the face side of the rail is pressed against the fence, the drill is centred over its edge.

Drill the three holes for the pillars in the top edge of the rail, and drill corresponding holes in the underside of the lower edge of the backrest. Repeat for the other chairs.

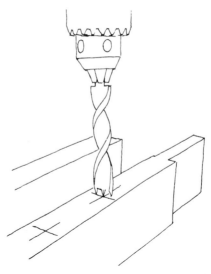

Now make a cardboard template of the backrest, taking the dimensions for the arch centres from the plans provided. Use the template to mark in the two arches in the back of each chair, then cut them out with a jigsaw using a T119BO saw-blade. Cut out the arches from all the backrests.

Sanding

Before carving the decorations on the rails and backrest, sand all the components carefully. Use a belt sander to remove the planing marks, and finish with an orbital sander mounted with 220 open cut sandpaper. While you are sanding, take care not to abrade any of the tenon shoulders.

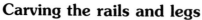

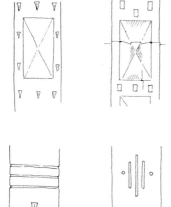

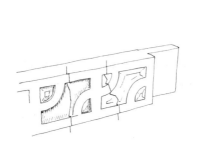

Carving the rails and legs

The illustrations show the different carved designs recorded from the original chairs. They are all based on straight cuts, incised with a flat chisel, or curved cuts, made with a knife.

Carving hints

Experiment with carving techniques on some scrap wood. Arrange a spotlight to shine at a low angle over your work, sharpen your knife and chisel, and clamp the work securely. Both the chisel and the knife should be held with both hands. The right hand usually applies the forward pressure and the left hand gives sideways control and restraint. Try to apply a consistent standard of carving, so you are not tempted to go back and upgrade work that has already been completed. Your aim should be to remove a shaving every other cut, without leaving any fibrous crevices or untidy bruising.

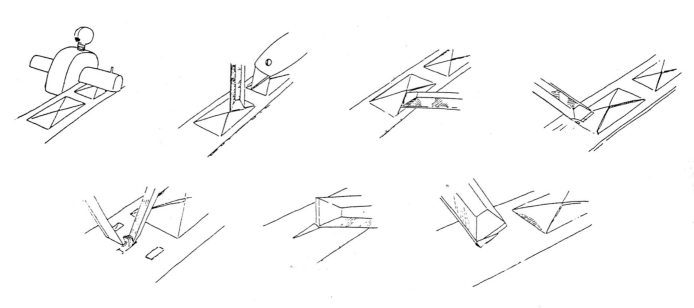

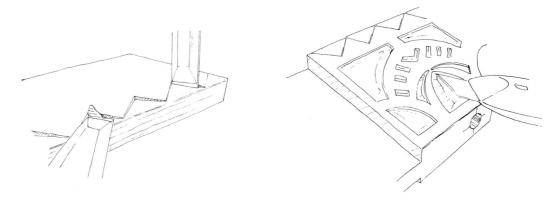

Do not worry if your curves are irregular and the straight lines wobble. The carving on the originals was capricious, and quite untidy; experiment for a short while, then mark out and start carving the front rails. When you have more confidence, carve the rail beneath the backrest. Then practise on some waste before carving the arched backrest.

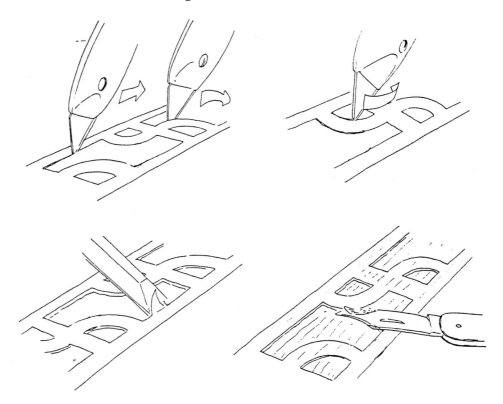

The series of illustrations shows some procedures for carving the main elements of the designs. When the carving is completed, sand the carved surfaces with an orbital sander, mounted with 400 grit paper. This will remove the pencil marks, without causing the carving to lose its crispness.

Turning the spindles

Three spindles are needed for each chair. Select an offcut of any convenient hardwood, and cut it into 1in (25mm) square-section strips, 4½in (115mm) long. Centre-punch the ends of each strip, and remove the corners of each strip with a chisel.

Tools

The tools you will need to turn the spindles must be very sharp. You will need the diamond point scraper, the curved scraper and the skew chisel. In addition, it will be a help to have a parting tool, or if you have not got one, a heavy-duty firmer or morticing chisel, about ⅜in (9mm) wide.

The design of the spindles is shown in the plans of the chairs. Make a marking tool to score the main features of the design onto the spindle, and place the first spindle between the lathe centres.

Setting up

Adjust the toolrest so it is level with and parallel to the axis of the work and use the diamond point tool to reduce the revolving spindle to a rough cylinder. While you are turning narrow spindles, it is particularly important to remove small quantities of wood at a time, and to hold the tools firmly against the tool-rest. This is a crude means of turning, and if you try to work too quickly, the spindle will whip and split.

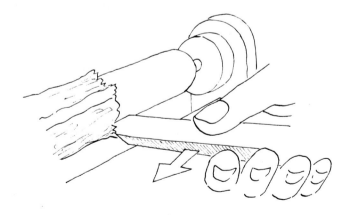

Smooth the cylinder with a few gentle strokes of the diamond point, and then sand it with a strip of backed 90 grit paper.

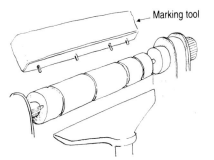

Marking tool

Keep the lathe going and, using the marking tool, mark the main features of the spindle on the revolving workpiece.

Use the skew chisel to incise the shoulder-lines as illustrated, then use the diamond point, followed by the curved scraper to shape the baluster. Finish the top of the baluster with the skew chisel.

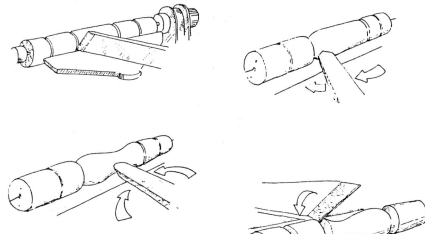

Sand the spindle again, this time with a narrow strip of 150 backed sandpaper, and finish by turning the ½in (12mm) diameter ends which locate in the holes in the backrest.

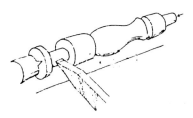

Remove the first spindle, and saw off the waste at the headstock end. Check that the spindle is the right length and fits between the backrest and top rail. Make any necessary adjustments to the marking tool before turning the remaining spindles.

ASSEMBLING THE CHAIR

Before gluing the chair together, make up a large number of pegs with which to pin the joints of the chair. The pegs should be made of the same wood as the chair, with a point at one end, more or less round in section for most of their length, but finishing square at the head. Each peg should be cut to the same length (1½in/38mm).

Pegs

The quickest way to make the pegs is to choose a wide strip of suitable timber, and cut a strip 1½in (38mm) wide from its edge. Cut several similar strips, so you will have plenty of pegs for the chair and some spare for breakages, then trim the offcut (again on the circular saw) so that it is little more than ¼in (6mm) thick. Chop these strips into sticks, no less than ¼in (6mm) wide, and then take each strip in turn and carve it to a peg shape as shown in the illustration.

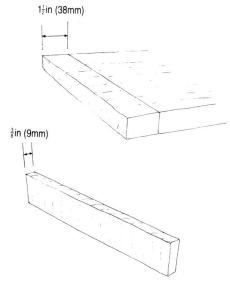

1½in (38mm)

¾in (9mm)

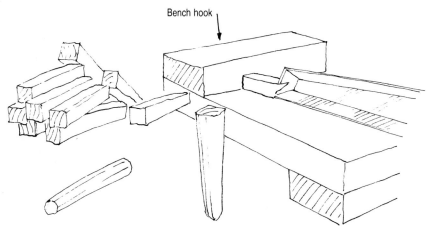

Bench hook

The advantage of splitting the sticks, rather than sawing them on the circular saw, is that they will be stronger and much easier to chisel, because the grain will run straight down the centre of each peg. To fit the pegs you will need a ¼in (6mm) brad-point drill, with a depth stop to prevent the drill going too deep.

Now check the piles of chair parts to make sure that each pile has its full number of components. When you have done this, select the four seat rails (two side, one front and one back rail) and chisel off their corners to leave them in the roughly rounded section as illustrated.

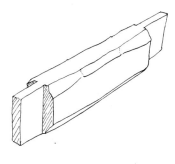

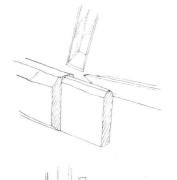

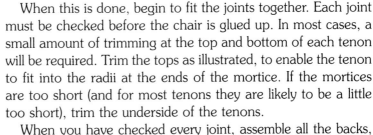

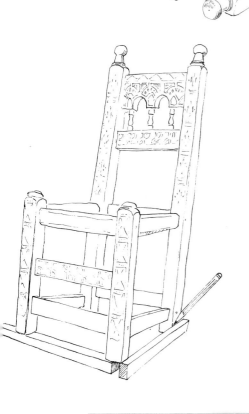

When this is done, begin to fit the joints together. Each joint must be checked before the chair is glued up. In most cases, a small amount of trimming at the top and bottom of each tenon will be required. Trim the tops as illustrated, to enable the tenon to fit into the radii at the ends of the mortice. If the mortices are too short (and for most tenons they are likely to be a little too short), trim the underside of the tenons.

When you have checked every joint, assemble all the backs, remembering to fit the spindles between the rail and backrest before driving the tenons into the legs. Although the spindles do not need to be glued, you should apply a small squirt of PVA woodworker's white glue into each mortice before the tenons are pushed in.

Fit the second back leg, and sight down the back to make sure there is no twist. Fit a string tourniquet at the top and bottom of the legs, and wind them tight. Wash away any surplus glue with a brush and warm water. Drill into each mortice through the back face of each leg, and hammer a peg into each joint. Leave the pegs slightly prominent.

Now assemble the front legs and peg them, then the four side rails. When you have fitted the side rails but before these joints are pegged, you should inspect and eliminate any twist in the framework by resting and leaving the chair on a flat floor.

When the glue is dry, place a 1in (25mm) batten beneath the front legs and, using a similar batten, mark round the back legs. Saw off the waste below the marks, and abrade the edges of all four legs with a rasp or rough sandpaper.

Waxing

Apply three lavish coats of soft brown wax polish to the chairs. Use a brush to clean the carving after the third application. For advice on waxing see page 103. Remember that it will be some time before the chairs acquire a satisfactory patination and colour. Short cuts to a good colour, using stains, paints and varnish stains, might prevent the chairs from developing a satisfactory finish later, so do not be disappointed by the appearance of the chairs. If they are used regularly, they will have improved beyond all expectation before the year is out. They will improve especially quickly if you have small children in the house.

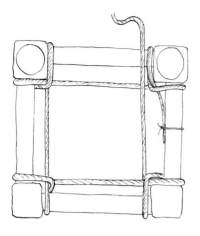

WEAVING THE SEAT

The chair seat in the photograph has rush seating. You can use rushing, rough twine, or a new product made from recycled paper, for your chairs.

The diagrams show different ways of weaving a seat. The first method is the conventional rushing technique, working from the outside rails towards the centre of the seat. When you are using a continuous string it is a help, particularly when you are reaching the centre of the chair, to cut the string into short, handy lengths. A simpler alternative is illustrated opposite.

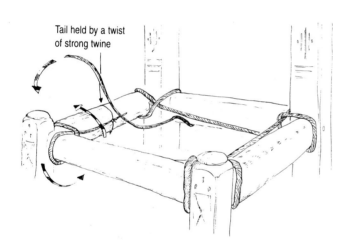

Tail held by a twist of strong twine

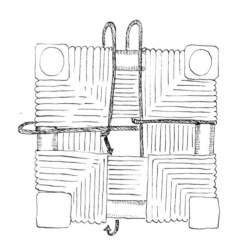

Tie the ends of the string together with one of the knots illustrated, positioning the knots on the underside of the seat.

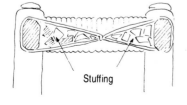

Stuffing

Tuck the tails into the space inside the seat with snippets of string and other dry wadding to make the seat firmer and more comfortable.

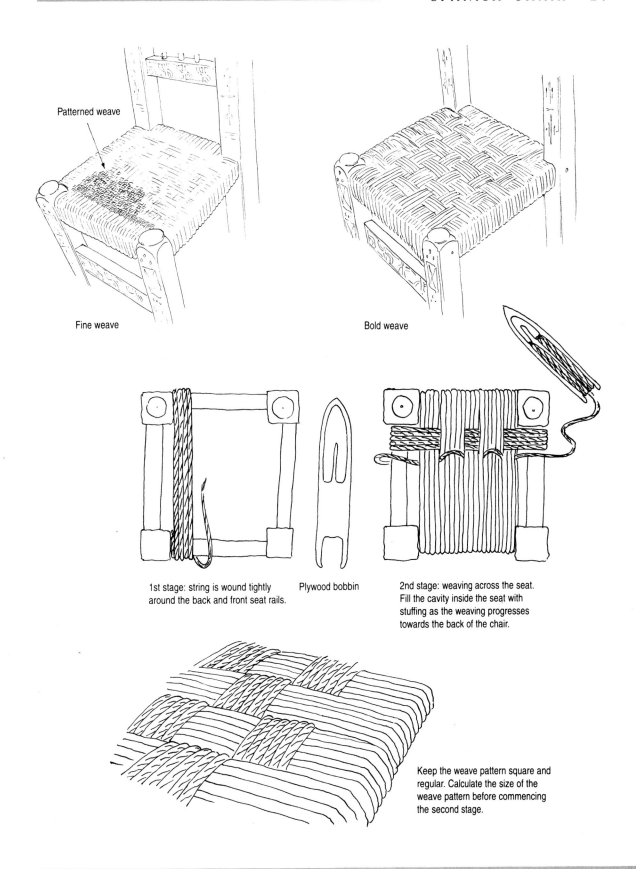

Patterned weave

Fine weave

Bold weave

1st stage: string is wound tightly
around the back and front seat rails.

Plywood bobbin

2nd stage: weaving across the seat.
Fill the cavity inside the seat with
stuffing as the weaving progresses
towards the back of the chair.

Keep the weave pattern square and
regular. Calculate the size of the
weave pattern before commencing
the second stage.

FRENCH SCULLERY TABLE

THIS IS A SIMPLE and attractive French-style country table. The top is clamped at the ends with cleats, which hold it flat while allowing some scope for shrinkage. The table legs are cut from 3in (75mm) square-sectioned pine, and the side and end rails are morticed into the top 4½in (115mm) of each leg. Below the mortices, the two inside-facing sides of each leg are planed to a slight taper.

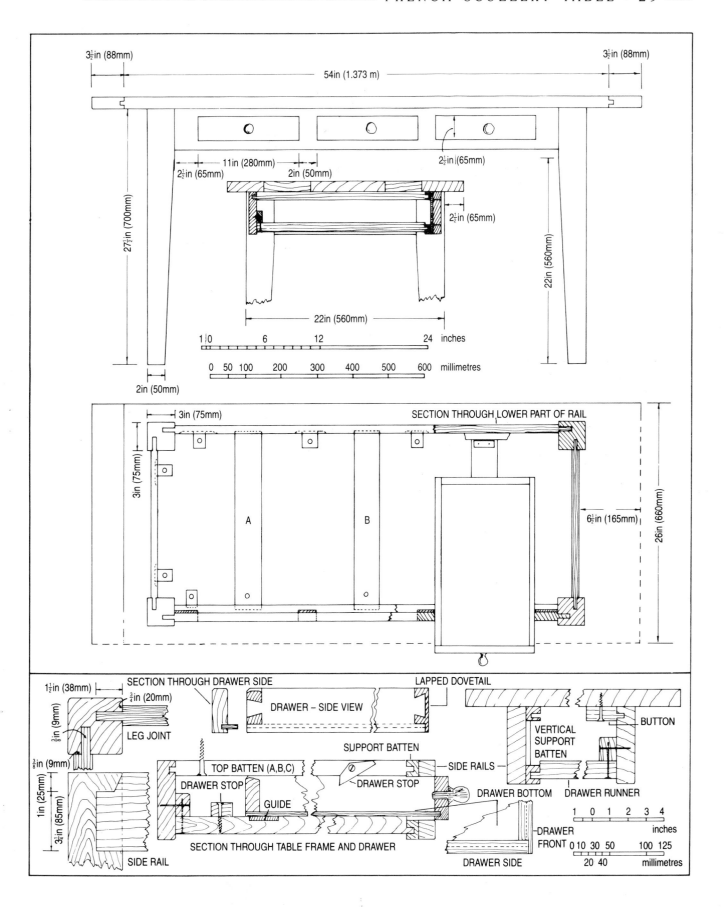

There are three small drawers in the side rail of the table which do not extend across the full width of the framework. They are only 2½in (65mm) deep, but despite their size they are useful, and can be fitted with partitions to hold cutlery, napkins, cookie cutters and other small kitchen utensils. The drawers are jointed at the corners with a single wide dovetail. An unusual feature of this table is the delicate frieze carved into the edge of the table top.

The table in the photograph (see following page 96) is made from larch, a strong, resinous wood, much used for fencing and farm gates. It is a rich orange red with a marked grain, quite hard to work, and with a lot of knots. It is a cheap, durable wood, and can readily be bought rough-sawn from country woodyards; it takes a wax finish well, and quickly wears to a beautiful soft sheen. The table has a waxed base, and the top has been finished with olive oil. Most other country woods would be suitable. Larch is probably the cheapest. Baltic pine, Parana pine and Norway spruce could be used, but it would take a long time for them to acquire such an attractive colour and interesting appearance.

TOOLS

Apart from the basic tools mentioned in the Preface, you will need a router fitted with a ⅜in (9mm) two-flute cutter, the home-made routing box described on page 15, and a good quality electric jigsaw with an orbital cutting action.

If you are using rough-sawn woods, an electric hand planer will enable you to smooth and level the face sides of the rough-cut timber very quickly. Concealed surfaces inside the frame-work do not need to be planed, but should be sanded with a belt sander to remove the worst roughness. The top is jointed with glued butt joints. For those without a pair of furniture cramps, the top can be pulled together using concealed tenons and pegs. Appropriate instructions for this are included in the text.

CONSTRUCTION

Select the wood for the side and end rails. The side rail into which the drawers are slotted should be virtually knot-free. Use a tape measure when you are selecting the wood to check that the pieces you choose for the rails are free of knots at the ends where the tenons will be sawn.

Saw the planks to the correct width. If both edges of the plank are wany, a straight cut can be achieved by guiding the hand-held circular saw against a straight batten, tacked to the rough edge of the plank as illustrated. After the first sawn edge has been planed smooth and square, trim the plank to a fraction more than its correct width of 4¼in (108mm) with the circular saw fitted with its adjustable fence.

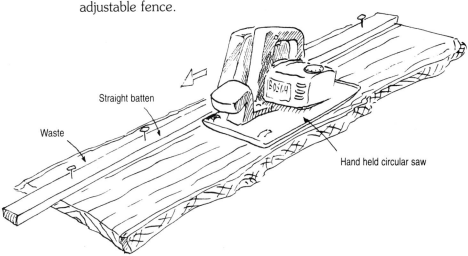

Straight batten

Waste

Hand held circular saw

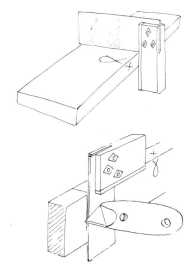

Plane the new edge straight and square, then plane the outer surfaces flat (see pages 143–5). Mark the face side and the face edge of each plank. These will be your reference edges when you scribe in the tenons and drawer slots, and they should be very clear.

The side rails and the end rails are the length of the exposed rail, plus the length of a 1½in (38mm) tenon at each end. Measure and cut the rails to length, then clamp the two side rails together in the vice, face edges upwards and face sides out-wards. Line them up before marking the shoulders of the tenons on the face edges. Now separate the two rails and mark around each shoulder as illustrated.

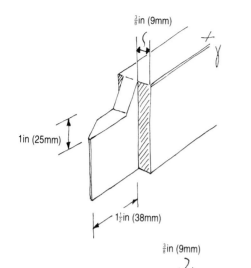

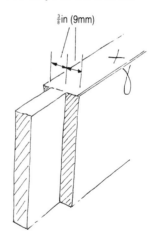

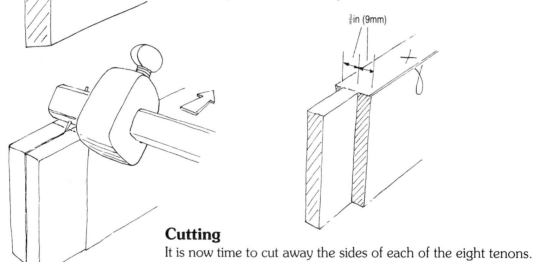

When the tenon is cut, it should look like the illustration. Notice that the regular ⅜in (9mm) shoulder is cut on the face side of the plank, and because the plank is of slightly varying thicknesses, the shoulder on the inner face varies from ¼ to ⅛in (6mm–4mm). In fact, it would not matter if there were no shoulder there at all, provided there is enough good wood in the rail from which to cut the ⅜in (9mm) thick tenon.

Using the marks on the face edge, square around the rail with a set-square and a sharp knife. A knife is better than a pencil as it will incise the shoulder-line, and should guarantee an accurate and clean shoulder cut. Repeat the above processes on the end rails.

The shoulder of each tenon is ⅜in (9mm) deep. Set a marking gauge to this measurement, and mark around the end and edges of each rail as illustrated, bearing the marking gauge fence against the face side of each plank. Reset the gauge to mark in the back face of each tenon in the same way as before, again using the face sides as your reference.

Cutting

It is now time to cut away the sides of each of the eight tenons. Using the clear marks you have made, saw the shoulder-line carefully. There are two hazards to avoid. One is the danger of sawing too deeply, and weakening the tenon; this can be prevented by sawing slowly, keeping the sawblade level at all times, and checking the depth of sawcut at the edges of the rail at frequent intervals. The other difficulty is in sawing cleanly such a wide tenon. There is always the chance, particularly when starting a sawcut, that the saw will hop and bounce, rounding and scratching the wood adjacent to the shoulder-line and spoiling the appearance of the work.

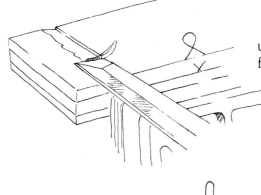

To prevent this from happening, hold the rail in the vice, and using a very sharp chisel, pare away a sliver of waste wood from beside the shoulder-line.

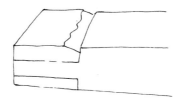

Now rest the tenon saw in the resulting slot, and slowly begin to saw. The teeth are already below the surface of the timber and, provided you work carefully, are unlikely to break out to score or damage the hard edge of the shoulder. Cut all the shoulder-lines in this way, then pare away the waste with a sharp, bevel-edged chisel as illustrated.

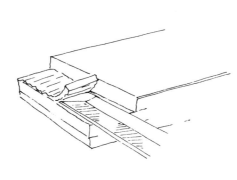

The mortices in the legs are stopped 1in (25mm) short of the top of each leg to prevent them from weakening the joint. A sloping haunch is cut into the top of the tenon, which matches the sloped recess cut from the top of the leg into each mortice. Cut all the haunches on the tenons, in the order shown, and then bevel the end of each tenon as shown below.

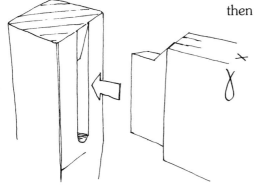

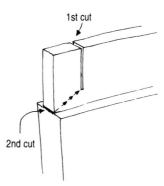

1st cut

2nd cut

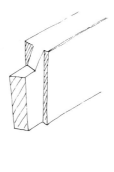

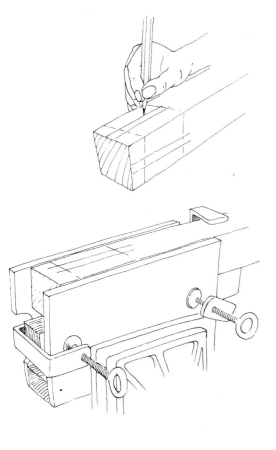

Marking and cutting the leg mortices

Cut the table legs from 3in (75mm) lengths of square-sectioned timber. Use a pencil to mark the lines around the top of the leg which define the top and bottom limits of the mortices, and pencil in freehand the position of each mortice.

The mortice is ⅜in (9mm) wide. Use a straight two-flute cutter of this diameter to rout it out. Mark the exact position of one mortice on one leg, as illustrated, then set the leg in the router box, and clamp it tightly in place. Insert the parallel fence attachment into the router base, and adjust the position of the cutter until it is directly over the mortice. Set the plunge stop to allow the tool to plunge 1½in (38mm), and then, holding the router in position, rout out the mortice by plunging the cutter along the line of the mortice. Do not try to drag the cutter through the wood to form the mortice. It is quicker to use the plunge facility, and you are less likely to overrun the ends of the mortice, or wander off course.

Routing the mortice

The first plunge of the cutter is unlikely to reach full depth because waste collects around the cutting edge of the straight cutter. So, when you have plunged the cutter right down the length of the mortice, return to the end you started at, and plunge the cutter to its full depth.

Rout out all the leg mortices then, taking each mortice in turn, cut out the sloping recesses at the tops. First slip the point of the tenon saw into the mortice and gently saw the sides of the recess, then remove the centre with a sharp ⅜in (9mm) bevel-edged chisel.

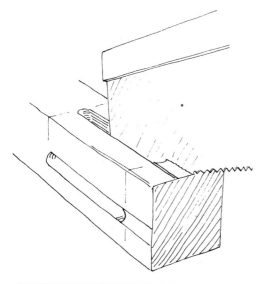

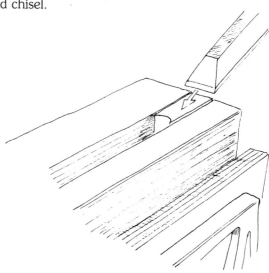

Fitting and trimming the legs

Number the legs and rail ends, and then try the tenons to see if they fit. They should be a tight push fit. If they are too loose, it is because your tenon cutting is inaccurate, and you may have to insert a shaving or two into the mortice to pack out the joint when you are glueing the framework together. If the joint is too tight, check that the mortice sides are clear of prominent ridges left by the rotating router bit. These might be interfering with the tenon, and can be trimmed with a sharp chisel. Look for other obvious faults: the mortice might be too short, or the haunch slope may be too narrow or shallow. These faults are easy to find and quick to remedy. If, after inspection, you find that the tenon is too thick, you will have to trim it. This is a slow job and frustrating – especially if there are several tenons with the same fault. Tackle the corrections in the following way.

Correcting the tenons

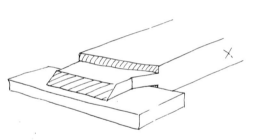

First check that the face side of the tenon is flat and set back from the face edge by the full ⅜in (9mm) width of the shoulder. This can usually be seen by inspecting the scribe lines around the side of the tenon, which should still be just visible. If your marking was a little indistinct, and you now have no accurate guidelines to work to, place the rail, face side downwards, on a flat board and try to slip a ⅜in (9mm) offcut under the tenon. If it does not fit, or it jams, trim it with a chisel. Try the tenon for fit again, and if it still does not fit, you will have to remove shavings from the back of the tenon. Mark the face that needs shaving, and put it to one side until all the other face sides have been checked.

The reverse sides of the tenons can be trimmed by chisel in the same way as the fronts of the tenons. However, there are usually more tenons needing their back faces trimmed, and it is often necessary to remove more wood from them than from the front faces, where more care tends to be taken.

Trimming with the router

The back faces of the tenons are easy to machine with the router. Set the router in its stand, and set the cutter to exactly the required height above the router bench (¾in/20mm). Lower the safety guard, start the motor and feed one tenon under the cutter. When half the back face of the tenon has been trimmed smooth and level, withdraw the rail

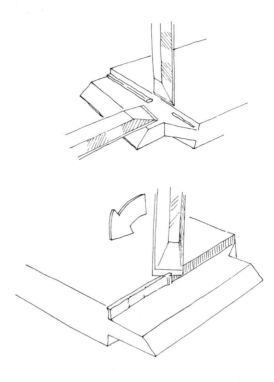

and fit it into the mortice. Adjust the height of the cutter, if necessary, before continuing with the remaining tenons. Keep the cutter away from the inside shoulder of the tenon and, after finishing the machining, trim away the remaining wood with a chisel.

All the joints should now fit. Inspect each joint in turn, making sure that the shoulder on the face side is tight against the sides of the leg. If it is not and you are certain that the mortice is of adequate depth, trim away the inside shoulder of the tenon, first incising a new shoulder-line with a knife, then trimming the shoulder back with the chisel held vertically. You should not need to make any adjustments to the face side shoulder.

Numbering the joints

Mark each pair of joints in turn. This is important, as you will not be assembling the framework for some while, and if you lose the marks it will take time to find the correct order for assembly. Mark the joints with a centrepunch or chisel, either on the tenons themselves or on the inside back rail, and on the inside top of the legs.

Pegging the joints

The main joints on this table are held together with wooden pegs. Correctly used, the pegs will draw the joints tight, eliminating the need for furniture cramps.

Take one joint at a time. Remove the tenon from the leg and, using the pillar drill fitted with a ⅜in (9mm) brad-point drill, bore through the mortice and leg as illustrated.

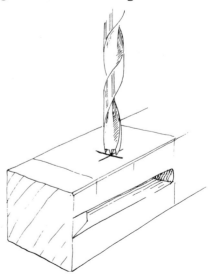

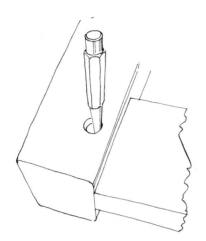

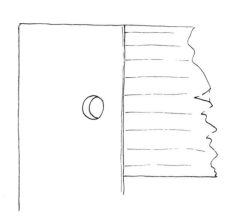

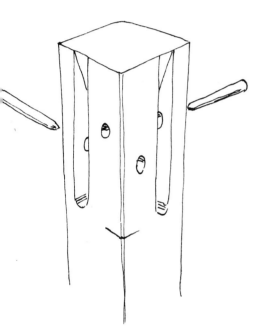

Insert the tenon, push it in tight, and punch on the tenon the centrepoint for the peg. You will notice that the centre is off-set, slightly closer to the shoulder of the tenon. Dismantle the joint, and drill a hole in the tenon, using the punched centre-mark. When the joint is reassembled it should resemble the illustration above right. Repeat this at all the other mortice joints, but remember to vary the vertical position of the peg holes on adjacent mortices. If the peg holes cross, you will find you cannot drive in the pegs properly.

Shaping the legs

Each leg is tapered on the two inside adjacent sides. These are the sides into which the mortices have been cut. Measure and cut the legs to length, first trimming the top of the leg flush with the top of the rail when the tenon is inserted, and then measuring down 27½in (700mm). Square around the leg with a set-square and pencil, then saw off the waste wood at the bottom.

Mark in the taper on the leg, running the taper out 1in (25mm) below the bottom of the rail mortice. Hold the leg in the vice, and plane away the taper with a hand plane. Lubricate the sole of the plane with candlewax every few minutes to ease the work.

When the first taper is complete, mark in the second and, holding the leg as illustrated, plane the second leg down to the mark. Round the hard edges of the legs with the plane, but do this lightly, and keep the radii small (less than ¼in/6mm). The final shaping will be left until the table is glued together, when the corners will be rounded off rather unevenly using a notched, hardwood stick.

Cutting out the drawer slots

The drawers are set into the straightest grained, knot-free side rail. Pencil in the outline of each drawer, noting that the drawers are set slightly above the centreline of the drawer rail. When you are satisfied with the pencil marks, incise them with a knife and cutting gauge (see page 139).

Bore a ⅜in (9mm) hole near the side of each drawer slot on the waste side of the line, then clamp the rail over the side of the workbench and, using the electric jigsaw fitted with a T301D blade, carefully cut around the outline of the drawer. Keep to the inside (waste side) of the line, and approach the corners in the manner illustrated.

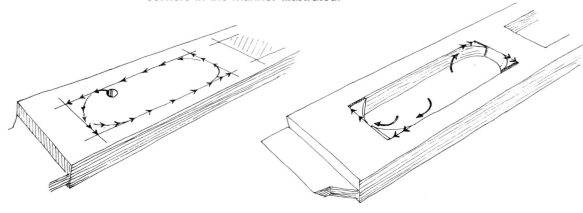

When using a jigsaw, particularly for cutting thicker stock, it can be a problem to prevent the tip of the blade from wandering off line. If your jigsaw is fitted with an orbital cutting action, the blade itself drags the tool forward, and the tip is less likely to deviate. When you are cutting straight lines, you should use maximum orbital action (this is adjusted by a lever on the side of Bosch jigsaws), and exert the minimum forward pressure with your hands. Just before you reach a corner, slip the orbital control to zero, finish the cut, then pull the saw back along its path, and cut a gentle curve to bring the saw back onto the new line and into the next corner. Continue round the drawer, and when the waste drops from the middle, set the orbital action to zero, and remove the remaining waste from the corners.

Cut all three drawer slots in the same way. Then use a file or a chisel to trim the holes, if necessary. Finish smoothing the inside edges with a block-mounted, metal sanding plate.

Side rail reinforcement

The side rail with the drawer slots cut into it is reinforced on the inside with ¾in x 1in (20mm x 25mm) battens. Four thin pine or plywood plates are glued behind the fragile, short-grain divisions between the drawers, and against the legs. The reinforcement battens are notched to fit over these. At the centrepoint of each drawer slot, the battens are grooved with a ⅜in (9mm) groove, 3in (75mm) long. These hold the drawer runners and top guides, which stretch right across the framework of the table.

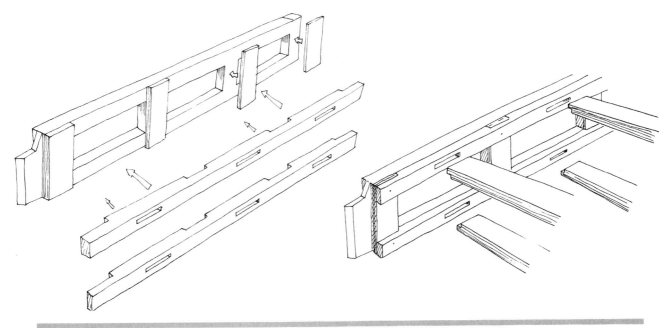

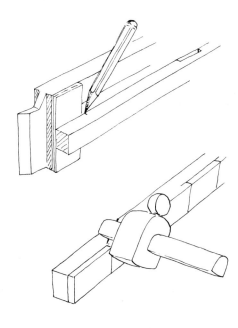

Fit, nail and glue the thin reinforcement battens, then cut the longitudinal battens to length. They should reach from shoulder to shoulder of the side rail. Line up the ends of the battens, then mark on the positions of the four thin plates. Remove the battens, square across the marks with a set-square, then use a marking gauge to mark a depth line for the recesses at each side of the batten.

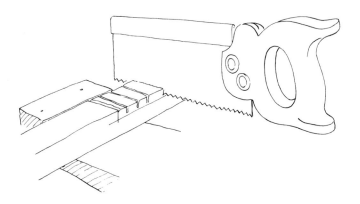

Make several sawcuts with a tenon saw across the face of the waste, including accurate cuts at each end of the slot. The additional cuts (which should not stray below the marking gauge lines), weaken the waste wood, which can then be removed with a sharp, bevel-edged chisel. Work inwards, first from one side, and then from the opposite, as shown in the illustrations.

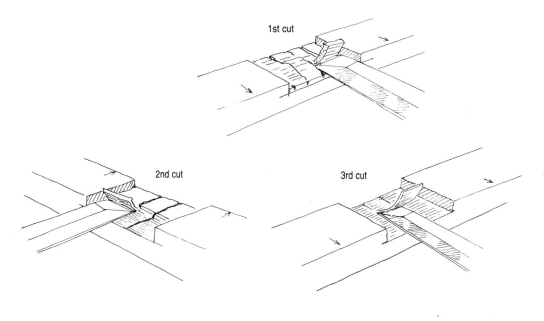

1st cut

2nd cut

3rd cut

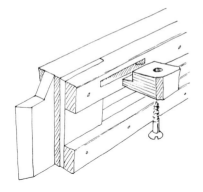

Place the battens in position, and mark on them the positions of the short grooves in the centre of each drawer. In addition to the grooves for the drawer supports, you will need two more grooves in the top batten. These hold the tongues of the buttons which are screwed to the underside of the table top, and hold the table top to the framework. Rout out the grooves, then glue and nail the battens in place.

While you are still using the router, mark and rout out on the inside top of the other rails the locations for the remaining buttons. Their approximate positions are marked on the plans.

Assembling the framework

First, make up a supply of straight-grained pegs to use in the joints. Select an offcut of timber, about 4in (100mm) wide, and split it into sticks about ½in (12mm) square. Using a sharp chisel, and bracing the point of the peg against the bench hook, trim the stick into a round, tapered peg. The peg does not need to be exactly round in section, it will look better if it has a few corners, or is slightly oval, but make sure that it has a point and that there is a steady taper in its first 2in (50mm).

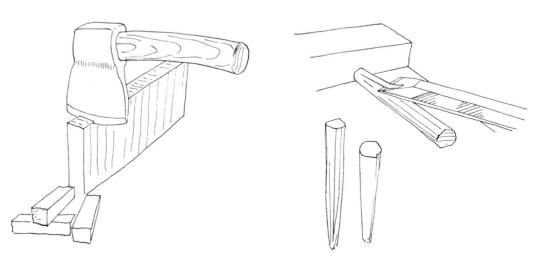

Now prepare the two side rails, checking that the correct legs are fitted onto the ends of the rails, and that the joints pull up properly. Lay out one pair of legs with the rail between them on the bench, face side up. Apply glue to the inside of the two mortices. A generous application at the top of the mortice will ensure plenty of glue is drawn into the joint as the tenon is driven home. Do not bother to run glue into the peg holes.

Press the two legs into position, then raise each leg onto an offcut of timber to bring the underside of the leg clear of the bench. Tap in the first peg with the hammer, burnishing the top of the peg as you hit it, slightly rounding the edges. Try to hit it all the way in. This will save trimming it later.

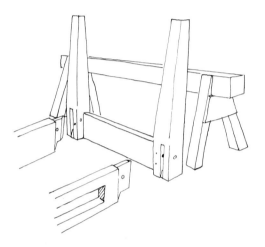

When both sides are glued and pegged, lift the rails down onto the workshop floor, top downwards, legs leaning against a bench or trestle. Fit the end rails and hammer in the remaining pegs to pull the framework tight. Sight down and across the framework to check that the legs are vertical and in line; some pushing might be needed to get them just right. Then leave the framework for the glue to dry. The floor should be flat and, as long as the framework is touching the floor at all four corners, it will be fine. It does not really matter if the table framework seems slightly out of square when viewed critically from above. Once the top is in place, no one will know.

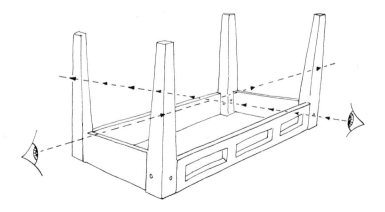

Making the drawers

The sides of the drawers are held to the ends with a large dovetail at each corner. The sides at the front are extended forward to conceal the end of the groove in the drawer front that holds the drawer bottom.

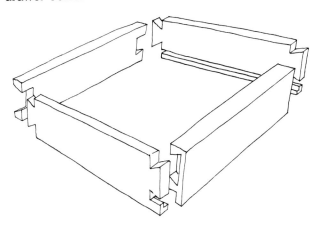

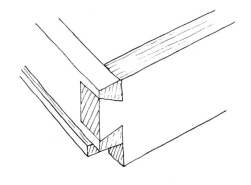

Cut out and fit the drawer fronts. Each drawer front should fit quite tightly. Subsequent smoothing and trimming will loosen the fit.

Number the drawer fronts, then cut enough wood to make six sides. The sides should be thinner than the fronts, but should not be less than ½in (12mm) thick, otherwise they will look out of place.

While you are still using the circular saw, cut enough wood to make the three drawer backs. These are ½in (12mm) shallower than the sides and fronts, because they rest on top of the drawer bottom.

Change the fence on the saw and, using the right-angle fence, cut the sides to length and cut the backs to the same length as the drawer fronts. Plane the tops of the sides smooth. Arrange a fence on the router bench and work a groove in the sides and in the drawer fronts, as illustrated. The grooves should be ¼in (6mm) deep at the sides, and ½in (12mm) deep in the fronts, and should all be the same distance from the top of the drawer (2in/50mm).

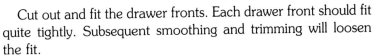

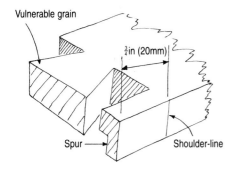

Vulnerable grain

¾in (20mm)

Spur

Shoulder-line

Marking and cutting dovetails

Dovetails are tricky to do well, but these are so large that mistakes probably will not matter much, and may even enhance the appearance of the piece.

Before marking out the dovetails, assemble the drawer components into piles: one front, one back and two sides for each drawer. Check that the sides are exactly the same length, and that the front and back are the same width.

The fan-shaped dovetails are marked first. Notice that the angle of the tails is sharp. The short grain at the outer tips of the dovetails will be weak and vulnerable until glued into the front and back of the drawer.

The front dovetails are stopped short of the front of the drawer, and are known as lap dovetails. They have to be big enough to hold the front, without weakening the lap at the front which conceals the joint. A straight spur conceals the groove cut in the drawer front. The shoulder-line of the dovetail should be ¾in (20mm) back from the end of the side. Incise the shoulder-line with a cutting gauge, then draw in the front dovetail and the spur freehand. With the cutting gauge at the same setting, scribe in the lap-line on the drawer front, and the shoulder-line and lap-line on the opposite side of the drawer.

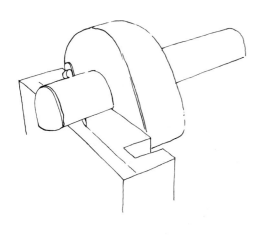

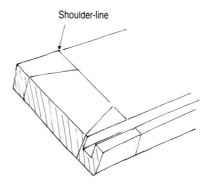

Shoulder-line

When you have done this, mark with a knife and set-square the shoulder-line for the dovetail at the back of the drawer. This line should be set back from the end ¼in (6mm) plus the thickness of the back (about ⅞in/22mm).

A single dovetail is cut in the side. The lower edge of the bottom pin must line up with the top edge of the groove in the side. The tops of the side and back should also line up. Draw in the dovetail freehand.

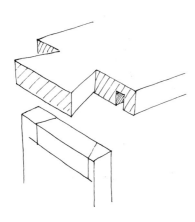

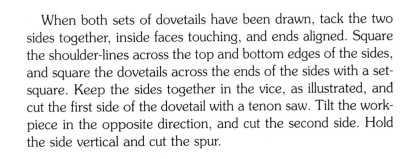

When both sets of dovetails have been drawn, tack the two sides together, inside faces touching, and ends aligned. Square the shoulder-lines across the top and bottom edges of the sides, and square the dovetails across the ends of the sides with a set-square. Keep the sides together in the vice, as illustrated, and cut the first side of the dovetail with a tenon saw. Tilt the workpiece in the opposite direction, and cut the second side. Hold the side vertical and cut the spur.

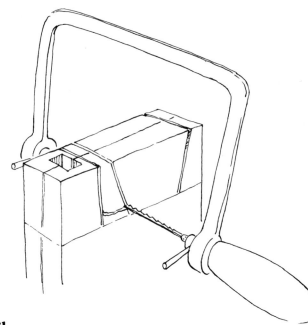

Sawing the dovetails

Now use the coping saw to cut out the waste between the spur and the side of the dovetail, as illustrated. Turn the sides around to saw the back dovetails. Square across the ends, and saw down the sides of the dovetail, holding the sides in the vice at an angle to allow the saw to be held vertically. When the dovetails at each end are sawn, separate the two sides.

Square across the inside faces. (When you have cut a few dovetails you will realize that you do not need to separate the two sides, as the sawing and chiselling can be carried out with them tacked together, but to begin with, it is easier to separate them and work with one side at a time.)

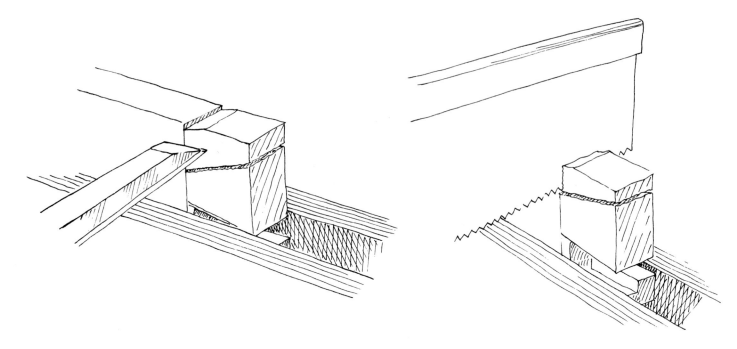

Cut out and finish the front dovetails first. Relieve the shoulder-line at the top of each side with a chisel, as illustrated above left, then saw down the shoulder to release the top section of waste from the dovetail. Lay the side flat on a piece of waste wood and, working first from the outside then from the inside, chisel back the waste to the line between the spur and the lower side of the dovetail.

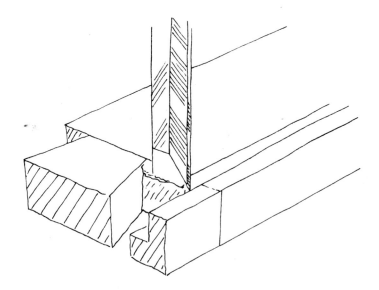

Now saw away the waste from the shoulder-line of the back dovetail, and repeat the trimming of the opposite side.

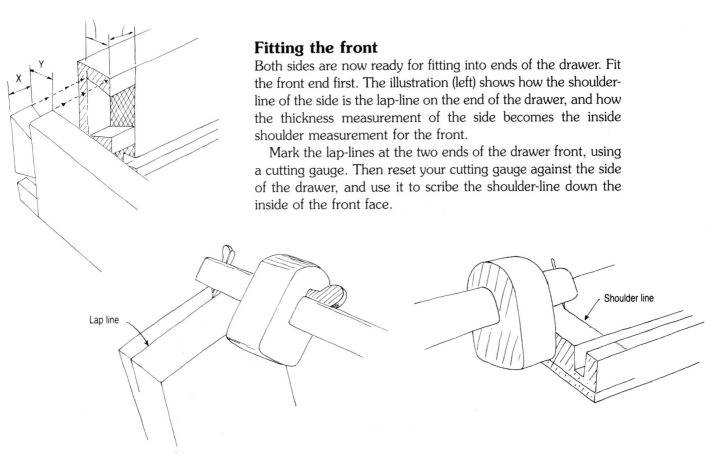

Lap line

Shoulder line

Fitting the front

Both sides are now ready for fitting into ends of the drawer. Fit the front end first. The illustration (left) shows how the shoulder-line of the side is the lap-line on the end of the drawer, and how the thickness measurement of the side becomes the inside shoulder measurement for the front.

Mark the lap-lines at the two ends of the drawer front, using a cutting gauge. Then reset your cutting gauge against the side of the drawer, and use it to scribe the shoulder-line down the inside of the front face.

Place the front of the drawer vertically in the vice, with its end just proud of the top of the jaws, and lay the side in position on top of it. This is how the joint will align, but in order to make it a very tight fit, nudge the side forward a little (1/16in/1.5mm), and hold it there tightly while you scribe down the sides of the tails and spur with a sharp knife.

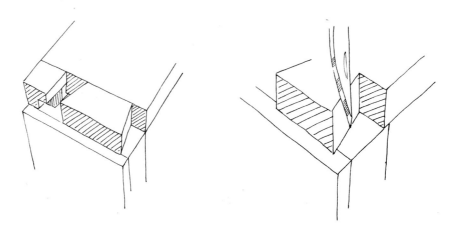

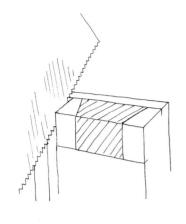

Remove the side, lift the drawer front out of the vice and turn it around so that the inside face is toward you. Using a tenon saw, saw down the sides of the pins as illustrated. They are such short cuts, that it is hardly worthwhile marking them out with a set-square, but you can if you like. Once the sides of the pins have been sawn, the remaining work is quickly completed with a sharp chisel, a mallet and a sharp penknife.

Place the drawer front face down on a thick wooden board, and clamp it. Then use a ⅝in (15mm) bevel-edged chisel to chop out the waste between the pins. Cut in the steps shown, stopping the chisel well short of the lap-line, and keeping it vertical.

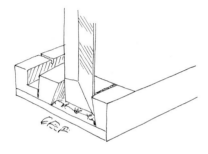

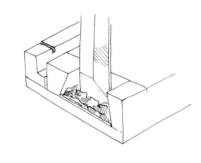

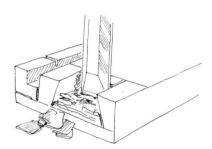

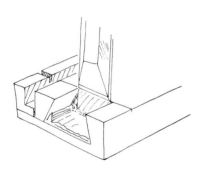

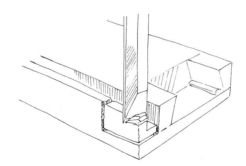

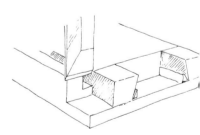

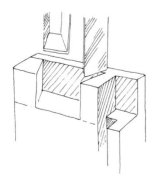

By enlarging and deepening the hole as you work toward the shoulder-line, the difficult-to-reach wood in the corners of the tails becomes weakened. Leave these corners until last.

When the cuts incising downwards to the shoulder-line have been made, place the drawer front in the vice and remove the remaining waste with the cuts illustrated. Trim the shoulder-lines level, and trim the sides of the pins and the face of the lap so that they are straight and vertical. If they are not, the dove-tail will split the drawer front.

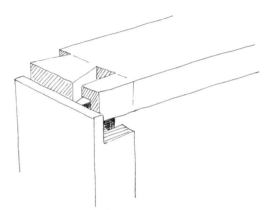

Now check that the side fits. Clamp the drawer front in the vice, and place the side over it, inside face and groove downwards. Inspect it to see if it will fit. Assuming that the shoulder-line and lap-line have been incised accurately, it is unlikely to be too loose. If it is, it will be because the pins have been cut too roughly, or the lap-line has been cut away. If the pins are too small, use a saw with a finer cut next time, or if you have not got one, offset the dovetail by a little more than the ⅟₁₆in (1.5mm) when you mark the pins, to compensate for the wood lost in the sawing.

Trimming

If the side is too big, check that the pins have been cut back accurately. If they are still too big, carefully mark and trim them back a little more. Do not touch the lap-line unless it is obvious that the shoulder measurement on the side is greater than the lap measurement. It should not be, because you used the same gauge for both measurements.

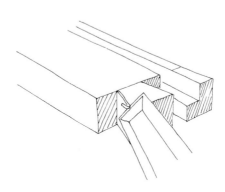

With a little trimming, the side should be ready for insertion. Before you do this, invert the side, clamp it to the bench, inside face upwards, and trim the corners of the tails, as illustrated. This will help them to slip between the tight-fitting tails. Tap the side into place with a light hammer, protecting the dovetail from uneven stresses with a batten.

If your first dovetail has been a disappointment, do not discard it: your next one should be better, and this one can be nailed in place. Do not do it now, but when you are about to fit the drawer together, collect some large-headed, rusty nails, and pre-drill the dovetail so that you do not split it. Clip the nails short, if necessary. When you assemble the side, conceal the worst of your work with a couple of nail heads, a few slight splits, and some bruised end-grain. A little soot rubbed into the brighter cracks prior to waxing will hint at bad repairs, not bad construction. Sharpen your chisels and knife before fitting the second lap dovetail.

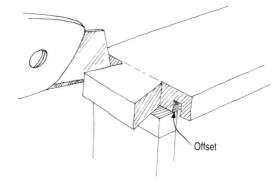

Offset

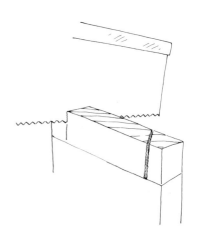

Marking and fitting through dovetails

The two through-dovetails at the back of the drawer are much easier and quicker to fit. The shoulder-line for the pins is the width of the side. Mark this in with a knife and set-square, or with the cutting gauge adjusted to the new measurement. This time the shoulder-line can be marked all the way round the back, because the dovetail passes right across the back plank.

Place the back in the vice, end upwards, and position the side over it, as illustrated. Once again, to allow for the waste in cutting, nudge the side 1/16in (1.5mm) across the shoulder-line, and scribe down the sides of the dovetail.

Lift the back and saw down the lines scribed on the end-grain. Remove the waste between the cuts with a coping saw, then, working first from the inside and then from the outside, trim the waste back to the shoulder-lines.

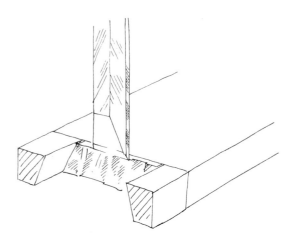

Test the fit and adjust the pins, then bevel the inside edges of the tail, and tap the side into place. Before dismantling this joint, fit the drawer front and opposite side, and take this opportunity to mark the set of pins on the opposite end of the back. This will prevent you from marking the second set of pins round the wrong way.

Drawer bottoms

When the jointing of the drawer sides is completed, cut the drawer bottoms to fit. These can either be made from 1/4in (6mm) plywood, or from solid planks, champhered on the underside to fit into the narrow grooves at the front and sides. Assemble the drawers with the sides, and check that they fit into the drawer slots. There will be a small width reduction after the joints have been glued and the pins are planed flush with the sides. If there is a major problem of width, the sides will have to be removed, and new shoulder-lines worked to, at one end of the drawer. It is unlikely that this will be necessary; it is much more likely that the drawers are being forced into the wrong aperture in the rail.

Gluing and fixing

When the drawers fit, glue the joints. Where necessary nail them together. Tap the dovetails together with a hammer and a light batten as before. When both sides are tapped home, slip the drawer bottom into position and nail it to the drawer back. This will hold the drawer framework square.

Fitting the drawer runners

Fit the drawer runners before the top is made and fixed down. As can be seen in the plans, each drawer has a central runner that bears against the drawer base. As the drawer is pulled out, it is kept in line by the sides of the drawer slot and two blocks tacked to the bottom of the drawer. The batten above the drawer runner is there to limit tilt on the drawer as it is pulled out, and doubles as a fixing point for the table top.

Select hardwood for the drawer runners. Cut the runners to length (remember to add the ⅜in (9mm) tongue to the length of the runner), and cut out the tongues as illustrated. Slip the runners in position, and glue and nail them to small blocks fixed to the opposite rail. Now cut and fit the top battens. These have a tongue at each end, and fit with a diagonal twisting movement.

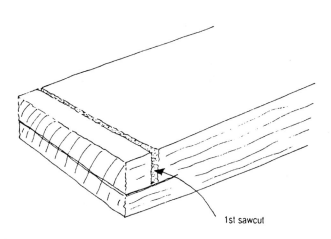

1st sawcut

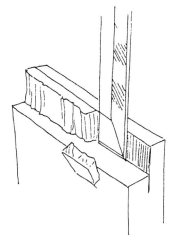

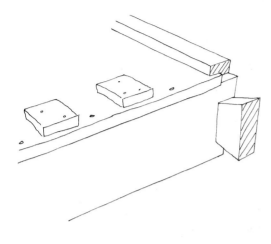

Slide in the drawers until their fronts are flush with the side rail, and mark the position for the drawer stops on the runners. Cut these out from a plank, and pre-drill them before screwing them in place.

Mark the position of the two guides on the underside of the drawer, and glue and tack them to the drawer bottom. They should not extend below the level of the sides. Lastly, drill and fit the simple drawer stops which pivot on the top battens. These can be made from any scrap of hardwood or plywood and are screwed in position. They work best when the table top is in place, but check that they can be pushed up out of the way of the drawer (from inside the drawer) and stay up so that the drawer can be withdrawn completely.

Drill the hole for the knob in the centre of each drawer, and whittle or turn the knobs from a 1¼in (30mm) length of hard-wood.

The top

Select your planks for the top. They can be knotty, different widths, and different thicknesses. Only the planks for the outer edges and the two cleats should be the same thickness, and planed on both surfaces; the rest can be left rough sawn on the underside, and need only rough sanding to remove the loose wood fibres.

Cut the planks so that they have two parallel, straight sides. A hand-held circular saw is ideal for this, first bearing its face-plate against a straight batten nailed to the waste side of the line (see page 31), then using the adjustable fence for the second (parallel) cut. If you do not have a circular saw, use either a handsaw (with ripsaw teeth) or an electric jigsaw fitted with a large-toothed blade.

When all the planks are cut to width, saw them roughly to length, allowing at least 3in (75mm) extra at one end of each main plank, and 1⅝in (40mm) on the end of each cleat. Plane the top surfaces of the planks flat. If you have an electric hand planer, work the plane along the boards, leaving a narrow prominent strip of rough wood between the shallow channels smoothed by the plane. After the surface of the plank has been planed once, use a hand plane to remove the narrow strips. If, in the initial cuts, you have levelled and smoothed the plank, reset the plane to cut a very narrow shaving, and plane it once more in strips, remembering to apply downward pressure to the front of the plane at the start of the cut, and to press down at the back of the plane as you reach the end of the plank. This will prevent the rotating cutters from scalloping the edges of the plank.

If some of your planks are twisted, plane down the high spots with the electric planer, and when these have been levelled, plane it from end to end in strips as before. Plane the underside of the cleats and the edge planks.

Joining the tops

The planks which form the top of the table are glued and butt-joined together. It will be a help to have two or three furniture cramps that are long enough to reach across and clamp the table together. If you do not have these, the top can be pulled together with hidden tenons. Instructions for fitting these are included on pages 54–6.

First the sides of the planks have to be planed straight. The easiest way to do this is to find a suitable machine-planed floorboard or piece of shelving, and use this as a fence against which you can press the router. Fit the fence to the router as illustrated, and lower the straight-sided two-flute cutter.

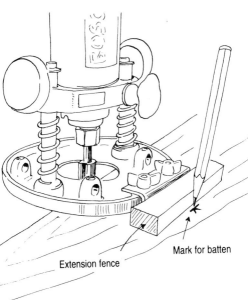

Extension fence

Mark for batten

Do not switch on the router, but pull it gently sideways, towards the middle of the plank, until the cutter touches the edge. Mark the position of the edge of the batten on the plank, and then repeat at the other end.

Clamp the straightedge to the plank, aligning it with the pencil marks. Check that the router cutter is set so that it will trim the entire thickness of the plank in one pass, then start the router. Move the router along the plank, pressing it firmly onto the surface of the plank, and keeping the fence tight against the straightedge. After one or two runs, the edge of the plank will be as true as the straightedge you have used to guide the router.

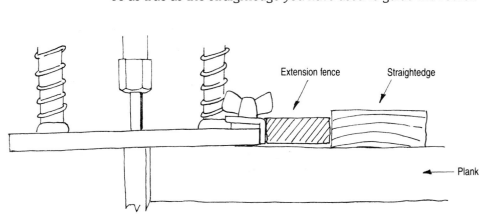

Extension fence

Straightedge

Plank

Unclamp the straightedge, and check it against the side of the plank you have just planed. If they are not a good, close fit, mark the high spots on the straightedge, trim them down with a hand plane, and then try with the router once more. When you have achieved one good joint, the others will automatically be as good.

Clamping

Fit the planks together. If you have furniture cramps, glue the edges and pull them together. Clamp two or three transverse timbers across the top to prevent the top from bowing. For instructions on gluing see pages 156–7.

If you do not have furniture cramps, tenon the planks together with two concealed tenons per joint. This will not take long, and will enhance the appearance of the table.

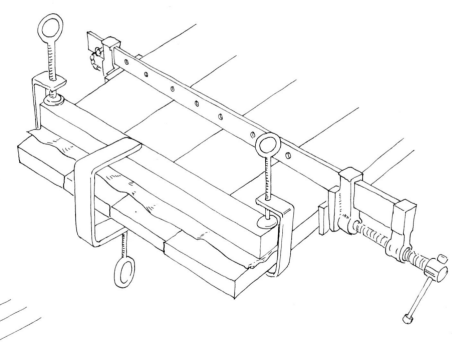

Pegging the table top together

Lay the planks together in their correct position, and mark the locations for each tenon freehand across the joints.

Take one plank at a time, place it in the vice, face side outwards, and plunge out the two mortices using a ⅜in (9mm) straight cutter. Repeat on all the other joining edges, using the pencil marks to give an indication of the minimum length of mortice required. Do not adjust the fence setting once you have started plunging the mortices. Now cut out a sufficient number of loose tenons from a piece of hardwood or ⅜in (9mm) ply-wood, and make sure that they fit in the mortices and allow the planks to be drawn up tight.

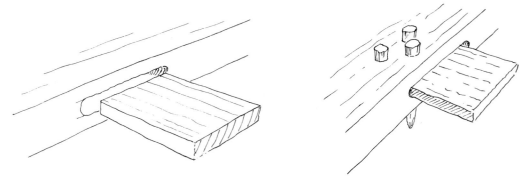

Separate the planks and tap the tenons firmly into one edge of each pair of joining planks. Drill through the plank and tenon with a ⅜in (9mm) brad-point drill, and peg each tenon with a pointed hardwood peg. Now drill through the centre of the opposite mortices. You will need to poke a slip of waste wood in the mortices when you are drilling them, to avoid weakening the mortice.

Clear out the mortices and press the planks together again. Indent the tenon with the centremark for the second peg. As with the framework pegs (see pages 41–2), this mark will be slightly offset so that the joint pulls together when the peg is driven home.

$\frac{3}{8}$in (9mm)

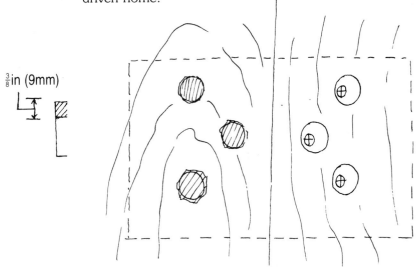

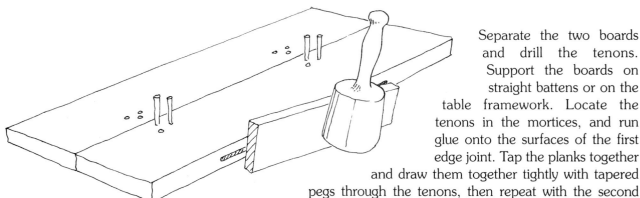

Separate the two boards and drill the tenons. Support the boards on straight battens or on the table framework. Locate the tenons in the mortices, and run glue onto the surfaces of the first edge joint. Tap the planks together and draw them together tightly with tapered pegs through the tenons, then repeat with the second plank. There is no advantage in trying to glue and pull together all the planks in one go. If you glue one at a time it will be easier to knock the planks together with a mallet and protective batten.

Fitting the cleats

The cleats are morticed and grooved and keep the top of the table flat. The groove is no more than ⅜in (9mm) wide and ½in (12mm) deep. The three mortices are the same width and 1½in (38mm) deep. Use the router box to cut out the mortices and the groove that runs between them.

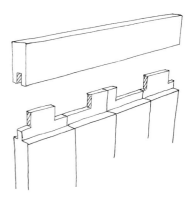

Marking and routing

Mark the position for each cleat on the plank top of the table. The cleats should be at right-angles to the sides. The diagonals from corner to corner of the top should be the same. Now mark in the depth of the tenons on the plank top, and cut off the waste with a jigsaw.

Use the same router extension fence that was used to trim the butt joints of the plank top, and guide the router against a short batten clamped to the top. Set the depth of the cutter to ⅜in (9mm) and cut away the top surface of the tenon and

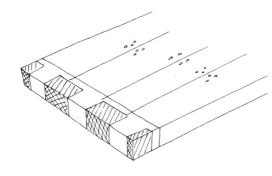

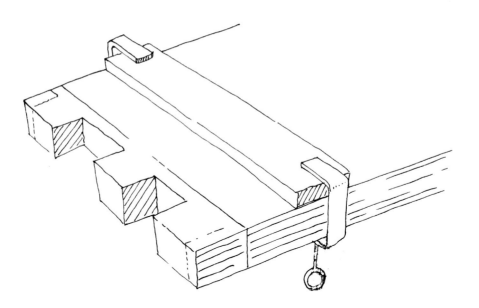

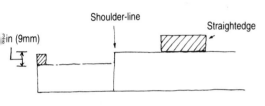

Shoulder-line

Straightedge

⅜in (9mm)

groove as illustrated. Work from the edge inwards, so that the router always has sufficient wood beneath its faceplate to support it properly. Turn the plank top over and, after resetting the straightedge, repeat on the opposite side. If the planks of the top are of varied thicknesses, you may have to make some adjustments to the depth of the cutter, but the extension fence should iron out most of the smaller irregularities in depth. Adjust the setting of the router until the tenons and tongue are no more than ⅜in (9mm) thick.

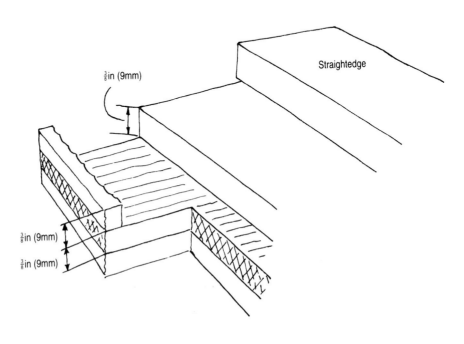

⅜in (9mm)

Straightedge

⅜in (9mm)

⅜in (9mm)

Pegging and trimming

Once this has been completed at both ends, bevel the end and the corners of the tenons and the outer edges of the tongues. Pre-drill the cleats for the pegs which hold the tenons, then assemble the top. Mark the centrepoints for the peg holes in the tenons, as described on pages 36–7, and drill them, before replacing the cleats and glueing them in position with PVA woodworker's white glue, which is slightly flexible and will allow the planks to shrink without breaking the glue joint.

Now mark and cut off the surplus wood from the ends of the cleats and plane around the outside edge of the table top. Work inwards from the ends so that the end-grain of the cleats is not split by the plane. Round the corners slightly and, with a keen chisel, remove the sharp top and bottom edges of the table top.

Carving the frieze

Before the top is screwed to the base, cut the simple frieze around its edge. Select a scrap of waste wood on which to practise. Take a large, sharp chisel about 1½in (38mm) wide and, using it freehand and hitting it with a mallet, make two incisions in the edge of the scrap in the shape of a pyramid, with the incisions deepest at the apex. Now use the chisel to lightly pare away the waste inside the marks. Two or three cuts will be enough to leave a well-defined shape. When carved in the edge of the table, the shadows cast by the indentation will look stronger. Now work round the table top, adjusting the size of the pyramids slightly as you near a corner.

Work especially carefully in the end-grain of the cleats. If you have difficulty here, stop and sharpen your chisel, and take very small cuts.

Fitting the top to the base

The top is fitted to the base with wooden buttons, as illustrated. Six or so buttons will be needed, made from any scrap of sound wood. In addition, screws are driven diagonally through each of the two centre battens which guide the drawers, one screw at each end, close to the rail. Drill the holes in the battens before putting the top in place. Angle the holes so that you can reach them with a screwdriver from underneath the table.

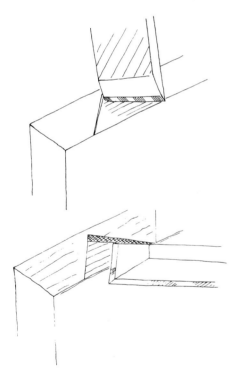

Set the table top on a pair of trestles and lower the framework onto it. Adjust it for overhang, then pre-drill the pilot holes into the table top, before driving the 1½in x 8 (38mm x 8) countersunk woodscrews through the battens into the table top. Fit the buttons where appropriate.

Smoothing the table top

The table top can now be finished smooth and flat with a belt sander, followed by an orbital sander. Advice on using these tools can be found on page 148. If you want the table to look old, dispense with the belt sander, and sharpen your hand plane. Set it to minimum depth, and lightly plane right over the entire surface of the table. Try to keep planing with the grain, and when you reach the cleats, plane along those. Lubricate the sole of the plane with candlewax. If the plane leaves score-marks or begins to tear up the grain, remove the blade and sharpen it again (see pages 150–52). When you replace the capping iron, make sure that it is screwed very tightly to the blade. If you still have problems, reduce the width of the plane mouth using the adjustment screws hidden beneath the blade, and retighten these very firmly before replacing the blade.

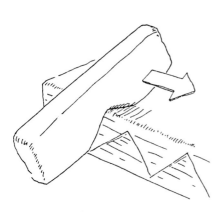

When the top has been planed, make up a rubbing stick, notched as illustrated, and rub it around the top and bottom edges of the table top, the lower edge of the rail, the inside and outside edges of the drawers, and the sides of the legs. This will burnish the corners, giving them an irregular, worn appearance.

Sanding

Now sand the entire table with an orbital sander, fitted with 220 open cut sandpaper. Follow with a finer grit paper on the top. Next, apply several generous applications of olive oil to the top. Leave the table in a warm room, and before going to bed on several consecutive nights, pour on a thick coat of oil. Wipe it away in the morning with a paper towel, or rag. This finish is water repellent, clean, and easy to maintain. Lemon juice will remove most unwanted stains from the top. Soy sauce rubbed into the wood will conceal any bleached marks. From now on, the table top will require one top-up coating of olive oil each year. Wax the base with three or four applications of brown furniture wax.

New England
Spice Rack

THE ORIGINAL spice rack of which this is a copy was made of pine and painted blue. This rack (see following page 96) is made of ash, tinted with a warm brown stain, and then wiped with a darker stain.

Apart from the frieze and the rail, the rack is made from ½in (12mm) thick wood. You will need a plank 3in (75mm) wide and 2ft 6in (760mm) long for the shelf. The ends are 8in (200mm) long and 3in (75mm) wide, but by snuggling the two sides together and cutting them with a jigsaw, you will need less than 16in (405mm) of plank for the pair. All the components can be squared and thicknessed easily and quickly using a hand planer with thicknesser attachment (see page 145). A tool of this type will enable you to take advantage of the great variety of rough woods available from country woodyards, allowing you to choose from many beautiful and unusual planks full of character, for your furniture.

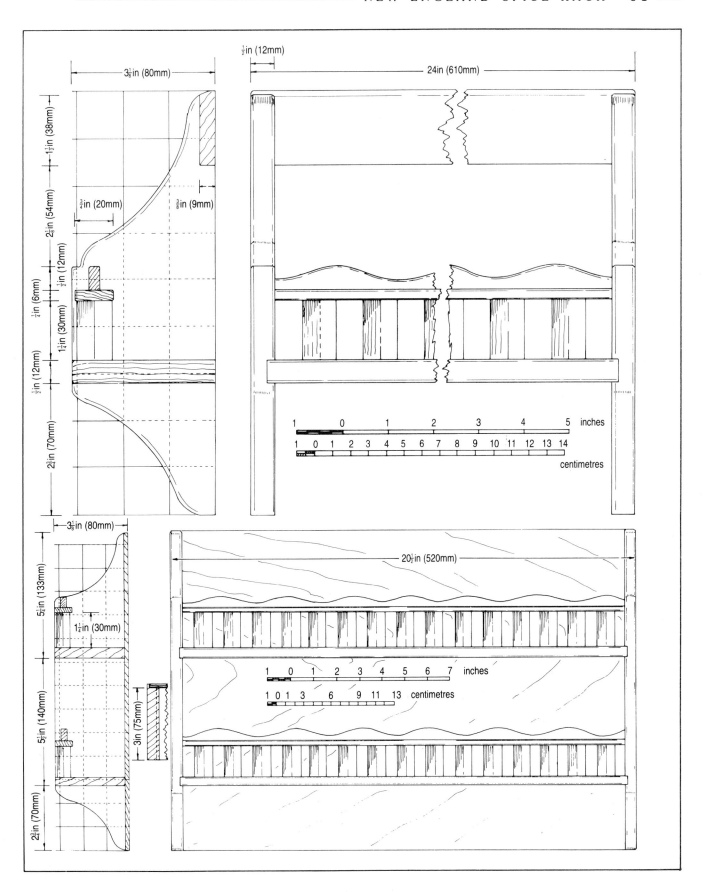

3⅛in (80mm)

½in (12mm)

24in (610mm)

1½in (38mm)

¾in (20mm)

⅜in (9mm)

2⅛in (54mm)

½in (12mm)

¼in (6mm)

¼in (30mm)

½in (12mm)

2¾in (70mm)

1 0 1 2 3 4 5 inches

1 0 1 2 3 4 5 6 7 8 9 10 11 12 13 14 centimetres

3⅛in (80mm)

20½in (520mm)

5¼in (133mm)

1¼in (30mm)

5½in (140mm)

3in (75mm)

1 0 1 2 3 4 5 6 7 inches

1 0 1 3 6 9 11 13 centimetres

2¾in (70mm)

CONSTRUCTION

Cut out the shelf, and mark off and square the ends. Trim them flat with the shoulder plane and shooting board, as illustrated.

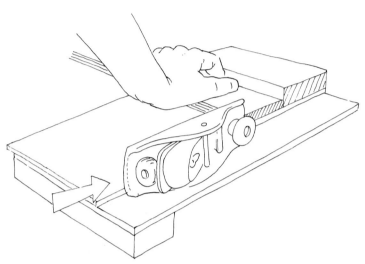

You will need to make a cardboard template of the ends of the rack. In the plans there is a 1in (25mm) grid superimposed on the side elevation. Reproduce the grid full-size on some clean cardboard, then refer to the plans and pencil marks on the full-size grid where you estimate the lines on the plans intersect the grid. Join the marks freehand and when you are satisfied with your enlargement, cut it out with a sharp knife.

Lay this template on the plank set aside for the ends, and experiment to find the most economical cutting pattern. When you have pencilled in the two outlines, cut them out using a jigsaw fitted with a T244D blade, which is ideal for cutting the small radius curves needed here.

Marking and cutting

Smooth the sawcuts with sandpaper backed by a board, or with a narrow strip of metal sanding plate. Place the two ends together, then measure and mark in the notch for the back rail. Measure and mark the sides of the groove which holds the shelf. Separate the two ends and incise the sides of the groove with a knife. Mark the depth of the groove on both end planks with a marking gauge. Now adjust the marking gauge to the thickness of the back rail, and complete the marking out of the notches in each end.

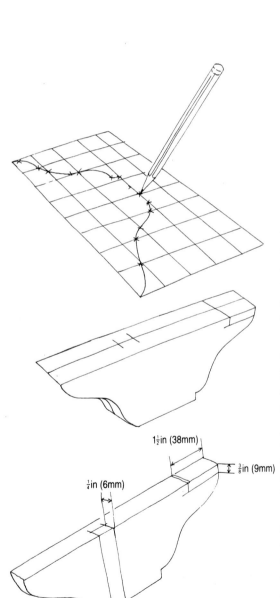

$1\frac{1}{2}$in (38mm)

$\frac{3}{8}$in (9mm)

$\frac{1}{4}$in (6mm)

$\frac{1}{2}$in (12mm)

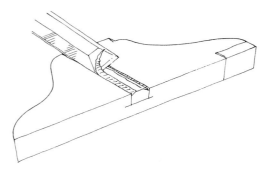

Saw out the grooves first. To do this accurately and cleanly, use a very sharp chisel to remove a narrow shaving from the waste side of each incised shoulder-line, as illustrated. Then clamp the side in the vice and slip the tenon sawblade into the shallow channel made by the chisel. Keep the blade pressed tightly against the line, while moving it slowly backwards and forwards. Apply a firm downward pressure, and keep the blade level and vertical. Do not cut beyond the gauge marks which mark the depth of the groove.

Saw the sides of the second groove, then trim away the waste between the cuts with a ⅜in (9mm) bevel-edged chisel.

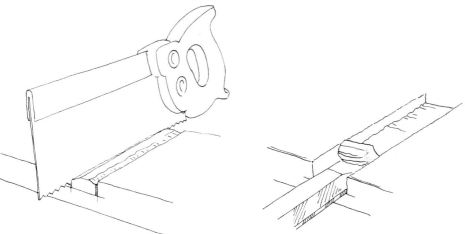

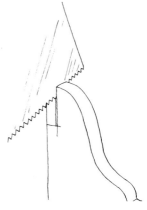

Now cut out the notches: two sawcuts are needed for each notch. Cut the gauge line first. Hold the end in the vice with its top 3in (75mm) above the level of the jaws. Take the tenon saw and, holding it at 45°, start the sawcut at the top corner of the notch, right against the gauge line on the waste side. Steady the sawblade with your left thumb and saw downwards very slowly. As the sawcut deepens the slot will guide the blade, and you can gradually raise the saw handle and bring the blade level to make the final strokes.

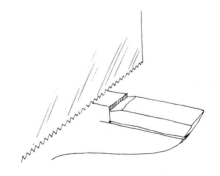

The back rail

Cut across the grain next. Relieve the line as shown, lodge the blade in the slight recess, and saw away the waste. Cut the second notch in the same way, and then sand the edges and sides of both ends.

The posts

Cut out and plane the back rail. Sand it smooth, working a slight radius on its front edges. Then cut out the narrow bar, ⅝in (15mm) wide and ¼in (6mm) thick. Plane it smooth, sand it, then remove its sharp corners with the plane.

Cut some lengths of ½in (12mm) square-sectioned stick for the posts, and plane and sand them smooth. They have to be sawn to exactly the same length, and the easiest way to do this is to saw them on a circular saw. Fit a fine-toothed blade in the saw, so that you do not splinter the posts as you cut them. Adjust the angled fence until it is set 90° to the sawblade. Lower the sawblade until about ¾in (20mm) of blade shows above the sawtable, and arrange a temporary short fence opposite the angled guide. This fence should not extend right to the sawblade, where it would trap the posts once they had been sawn off. Instead it is used as a stop, against which the freshly sawn end of the stick is pressed. This will guarantee that your posts are all the same length.

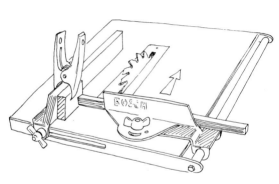

The frieze

The frieze can be cut with a fretsaw or with a coping saw, but it is easier to cut it with a jigsaw fitted with a fine T244D blade. If you are using a jigsaw, you will need to cut the frieze from some ½in (12mm) thick wood, correcting the thickness later. This prevents it from whipping as the jigsaw cuts into it. If you are making the rack with two shelves, as illustrated on the plans, the two friezes can be cut simultaneously by drawing the frieze down the centre of a suitable board, and using both strips separated by the saw.

Draw the frieze freehand, keeping inside the parallel guidelines ruled on the face of the board. You can use a template for this if you wish, but minor irregularities in the curves do not matter, as long as the tops of the bumps are in line. Clamp the board in the vice, and saw it in one sawcut, running the length of the frieze. When the jigsaw reaches the vice, the blade will begin to jam. When this happens, stop the saw, withdraw the blade, and move the wood along in the vice. Slip the blade back

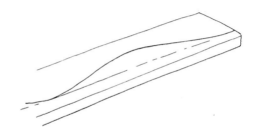

into the sawcut and continue cutting. As you reach the end of the frieze you will have to stop the saw again and move the board back into the vice, so that the uncut end extends beyond the jaws. Clamp the vice tightly, and continue to use the jigsaw in the same direction as before. It is best not to start from the ends and work towards the centre because if the blade wanders slightly from the vertical, the cuts from the opposite ends may not join up.

Plane the face of the frieze and then trim it to width with the circular saw. Plane the inside faces, and sand the tops of the friezes. Sand every component thoroughly to remove all surface roughness. Use 220 grit paper backed by a hard foam pad, rubbing with the grain. Use the paper to remove any remaining hard edges from the sides of the posts, the sides and the frieze.

ASSEMBLY

The rack is glued and nailed together. Use panel pins to hold the sides to the shelf and back rail, and snipped off panel pins to secure the posts and frieze.

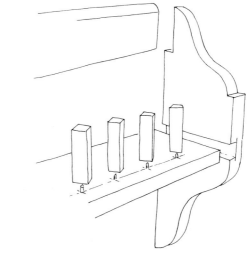

Fit a fine drill bit into the pillar drill, and drill a couple of pilot holes through the centre of the groove. Repeat at the opposite end. Squirt a little PVA woodworker's white glue into the groove at one end. Fit the shelf into it, align its front edge and drive two panel pins into the end-grain of the shelf. Fit the

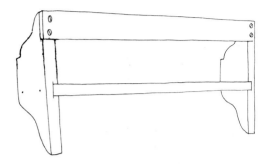

opposite end in the same way. Glue and screw the back rail to the ends to stabilize the rack.

Now make the simple jig shown in the illustration, and use it to position and hold the panel pins while you drive them into the top edge of the shelf. Remember that whenever you are hitting or nailing your work you must support it properly. When you are hammering in the pins, the shelf can be supported on the corner of a table. Cut off the heads of the pins before repositioning the jig. This should guarantee accurate and regular spacing.

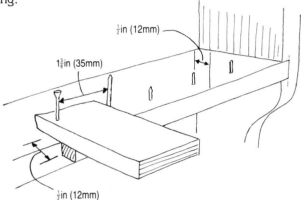

$\frac{1}{2}$in (12mm)

$1\frac{3}{8}$in (35mm)

$\frac{1}{2}$in (12mm)

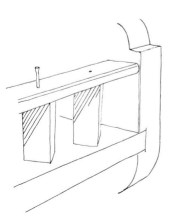

Take one post at a time, drop a spot of glue around the nail, and tap the post onto the nail, positioning it at 45° to the front edge of the shelf. Repeat with the other posts.

Trim the bar which sits above the posts to length. Apply a spot of glue to the top of each post, position the bar with its front edge slightly overhanging the front corners of the posts, and nail it in position.

Bring the rack up the right way again, and glue and pin the top frieze to the top of the bar. Screw two mirror plates onto the back rail after the rack has been stained and polished.

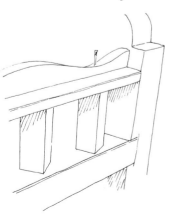

FINISHING

The rack featured in the photograph is made of ash, and was stained as follows. First apply a coat of warm brown Colron stain. A mixture of American Walnut and English Light Oak will be ideal. Apply this quickly onto all the surfaces using a narrow brush. Wipe away excess stain with a cotton rag.

Without waiting for the stain to dry, mix equal quantities of shellac (button polish) and methylated spirits, and brush this dilute and quick-drying polish all over the spice rack. The shellac will take about 40 minutes to dry. When it is dry, smooth the sealed surfaces by rubbing them lightly with 0000 wire wool. Then take some Jacobean Dark Oak stain and a clean cloth and apply the dark stain briskly over the sealed surfaces. Dab or wipe the stain away in places to highlight the richer tones beneath, and then leave the stain to dry. After an hour, you can brush a coat of undiluted shellac polish over the rack and leave it to dry.

After you have applied three or four coats of shellac, and given the polish plenty of time to dry, smooth the surfaces by rubbing them with a tight wad of 0000 wire wool. Unclog the wool every few moments by tapping or flicking it with your fingers. Avoid rubbing too hard at the corners so that you do not scrape away the polish and stain and reveal the light timber. Complete the finishing with brown furniture wax.

There are modifications in the plans, in case you want a larger rack with an alternative end outline, into which two shelves and a thin backboard are recessed. On this model there is no top rail. The rack is suspended by two screws driven through the backboard. Rebate the backs of the ends using the router fitted with a ⅜in (9mm) cutter, as described on page 149. The order of construction for both racks is the same.

PLATE RACK

THIS PLATE RACK (see photograph following page 96) is made from
yew wood, with larch planks at the back. It is designed to hold
and display plates and platters. An unusual feature is the long topboard, which forms an extra shelf for casseroles and pots.

You should choose interesting wood for this rack. Because it is
used for displaying the family plates, it will attract a lot of attention.

This is not a difficult rack to make nor will it take long if you have
a router and a bench-mounted circular saw. As you can see in the
plans, the shelves fit into stopped housings routed in the sides. The
bottom shelf is pegged to the sides and the front rail, and the narrow
stringers which retain the plates are tenoned into the sides of the
rack, and pegged. The back planks are nailed into the rebates in the
sides. The top plank is slotted onto the sides, and nailed into the
sides from the top where no one can see the nailheads.

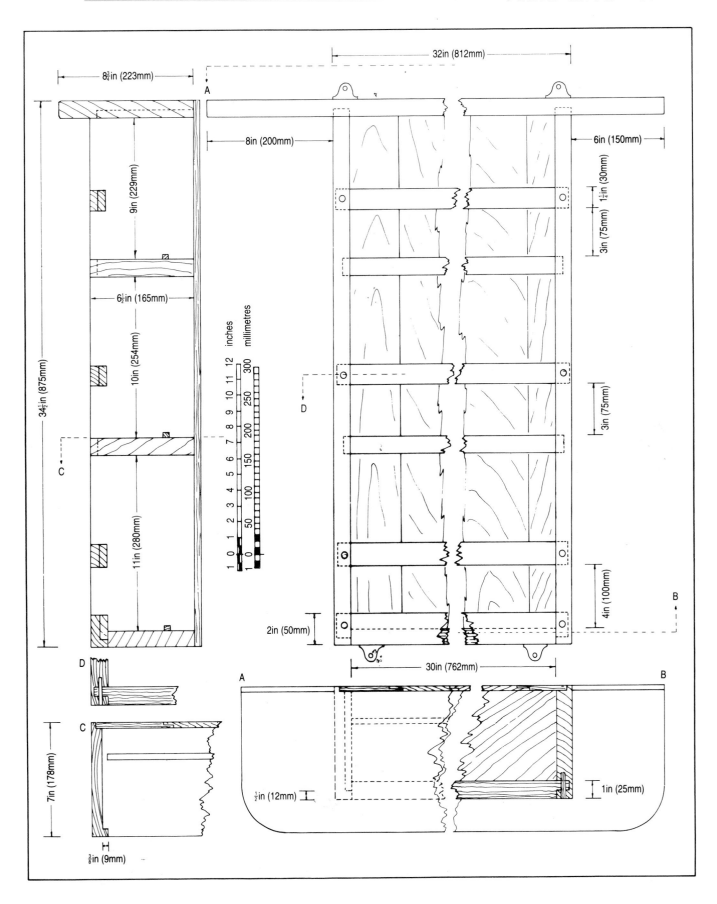

CONSTRUCTION

Select woods that have an unusual or interesting appearance. Freshly machined pine or spruce will not be suitable, unless the rack is going to be painted. Fruitwood, yew wood, poplar or birch will all be satisfactory. Use the most beautiful planks for the sides of the rack.

Cut the components to size. The bottom shelf is narrower than the others because it fits between the front rail and the backboard. The top plank is 2in (50mm) wider than the sides, and the middle two shelves are narrower than the sides by the depth of the side rebates.

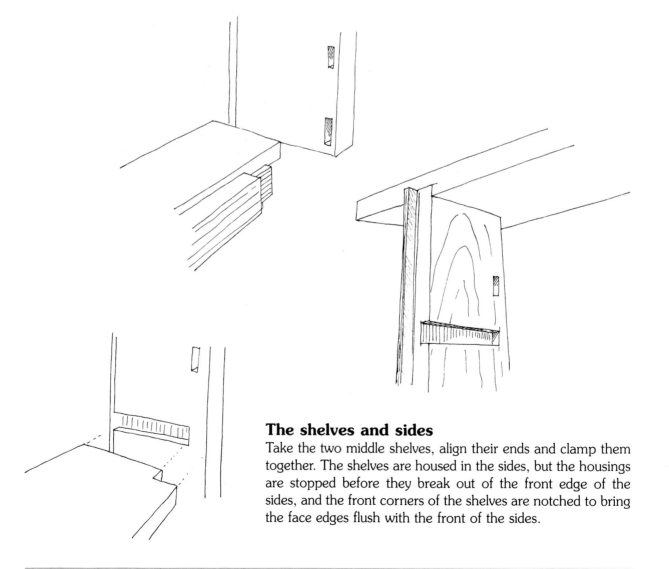

The shelves and sides
Take the two middle shelves, align their ends and clamp them together. The shelves are housed in the sides, but the housings are stopped before they break out of the front edge of the sides, and the front corners of the shelves are notched to bring the face edges flush with the front of the sides.

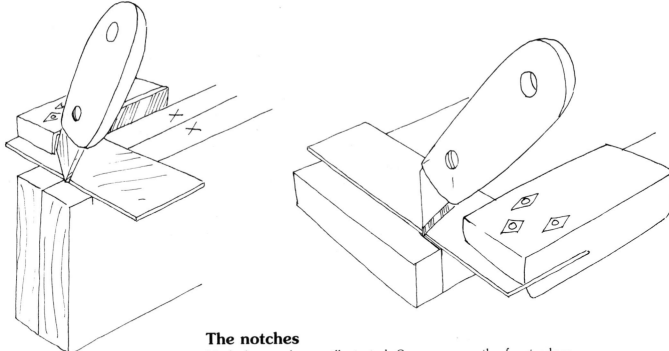

The notches

Mark the notches as illustrated. Square across the front edges of the shelves with a set-square and knife to mark the depth of the housing at each end, then separate the shelves. Resting the set-square against the face edge, square back to complete the cutting line for the notch. Use a marking gauge to scribe in the shoulder mark.

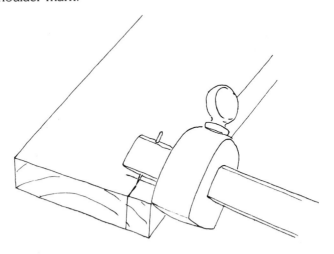

Saw out the notches; first relieve the lines on the waste side of the notches with a chisel (see page 140), then saw down to the scribed line. Now turn the shelf in the vice, and either saw or chisel off the waste.

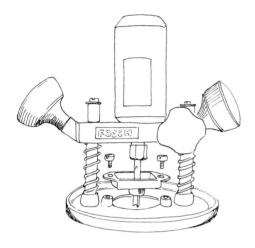

Marking the side housings

Clamp the two sides together and mark in the positions for the shelves and stringers. Make all these marks on the inside face of the shelves with a sharp pencil. The lines must be accurately defined, even though the housings and mortices are cut by router. It is not necessary to incise the pencil marks with a knife.

The template guide

Fit the template guide to the faceplate of the router, and fit the largest possible straight router cutter that can be plunged through the guide. A ¼in (6mm) cutter is large enough for cutting the housings, but template guides that take larger diameter cutters are supplied by most router manufacturers, and are worth buying if you are planning to do a lot of woodwork. If you are unable to buy a router guide, then your suppliers may be able to sell you a sub-base plate, and this can be fitted with a range of guide plates.

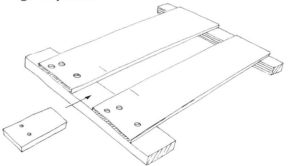

Make the template for cutting the housings. All the housings are identical and this simple guide can be used for all of them. Once in position it is nailed to the inside surface of the side. Use a scrap piece of wood to test the template and the router settings before cutting out the housings on the two sides.

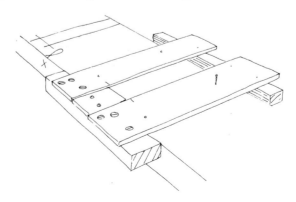

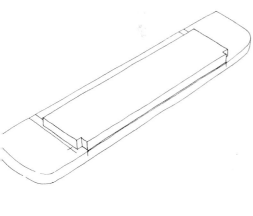

The top

Take the shelves and check that the notches you have sawn on them match the housings marked on the underside of the top. If they do not, move one set of housing marks until they do. Cut out the housings on the underside of the top.

Clamp the router in the router bench, and fit it with a ⅜in (9mm) straight cutter. Rout out the rebates in the backs of the sides. Now readjust the fence of the router bench, and rout out the mortices in the sides of the rack, stopping the mortices ⅛in (4mm) short of the full thickness of the sides. Use a ⅜in (9mm) chisel to square the ends of the mortices, as illustrated.

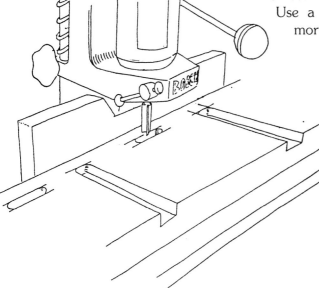

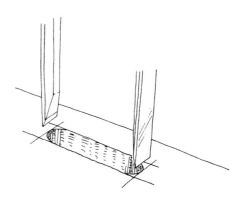

The tenons

The stringers and the bottom rail are the same length. They have the same length of tenons at each end, and the dimensions between the shoulders are identical. Mark the shoulders of the stringers and rail with the pieces stacked together, then use the marking gauge to scribe the face of the tenon as illustrated.

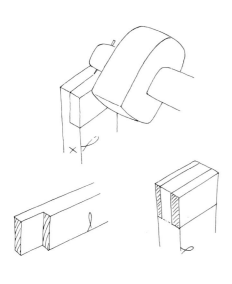

The tenons shown in the plans are all bare-faced. If you have a shoulder on each side of the tenon, you will have to adjust the marking gauge a second time, marking the inner face of the tenon in a separate operation. Cut and fit the tenons. Instructions for cutting tenons (including the use of a router and a circular saw) can be found on pages 16–18.

Sand each piece of wood thoroughly. The backboards have not been fitted yet, and can be left until later.

ASSEMBLY

Fit all the tenon joints together, run a small quantity of PVA woodworker's white glue into each housing and slide the shelves into place. Drive one nail through the end of each shelf to hold the rack together while the glue dries. Punch the nailheads below the surface so they can be hidden later.

Squirt some glue into the housings grooved in the underside of the top plank, and tap the top plank into position on top of the sides. This will hold the sides steady, and two more nails driven through the top into the end of each side will give the rack even more rigidity. Wipe away any excess glue with a clean rag and leave the glue to harden.

Now fit the bottom shelf. This has to be glued and clamped to the front rail, and is held at the sides with wooden pegs. Glue the front edge first, then when the glue has dried, tip the rack on its side and drill two or three holes on each side for the pegs. Trim the pegs to size and length. They need to be a fairly tight fit in the holes, but they can flare a little at the tops. Each peg

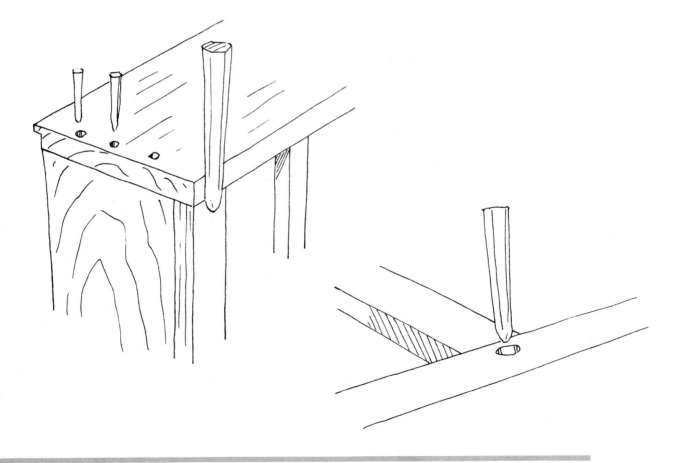

must be exactly the right length. If you can, you should try to avoid cutting the pegs off after fitting, as the sawing might damage the sanded surfaces. Squirt a little glue into the rim of each hole and tap the pegs in place.

Despite your best intentions, some of the pegs will have to be trimmed. Saw them to length with a sharp hacksaw blade, and protect the surfaces by slipping a postcard over the prominent peg before sawing. Trim the peg with a very sharp chisel, working from the sides of the peg to its centre.

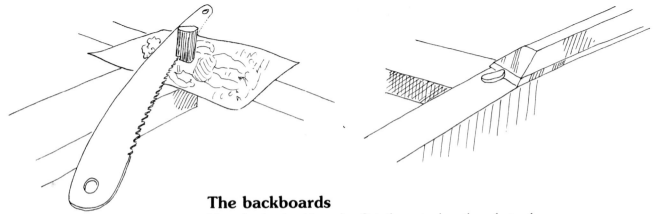

The backboards

Now fit the backboards. Cut them to length, rebate them so that they fit together as illustrated, and nail them to the sides and the back of the shelves. Fit the two small additional pieces to the back of the topboard to bring its back edge flush with the sides and back of the rack. Screw the two brass mirror plates to the back of the rack at the top, and another pair of plates to the base. This is quite a heavy piece of furniture, so you will probably have to enlarge the holes in the mirror plates to take the 2in x 10 gauge (50mm x 10) roundheaded screws required to hold it to the wall.

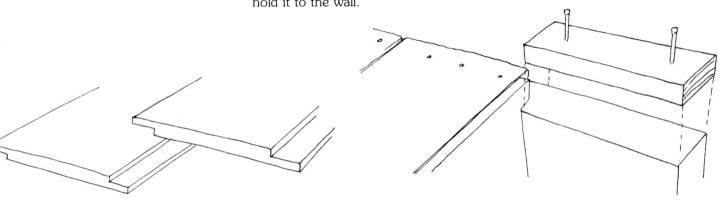

FINISHING

Sand the rack with the 220 grit open cut paper. The example featured in the photograph is made of yew wood which has been washed with a dilute coat of tannic acid, left to dry, lightly sandpapered, and then 'fumed' in a clear polythene bag containing a saucer of ammonia. The ammonia reacts with the tannic acid in the wood, turning the wood a rich, warm brown.

The advantage of this method is that dramatic colour changes can be achieved without overloading the wood with stain, which tends to obliterate the clarity of the grain. But fuming is difficult to control, and you must keep a close watch to ensure that the colour changes are even. It is sometimes necessary to open the fuming bag and replenish the ammonia, or move the dish to another area. The wood that is nearest the ammonia will darken more quickly than that further away.

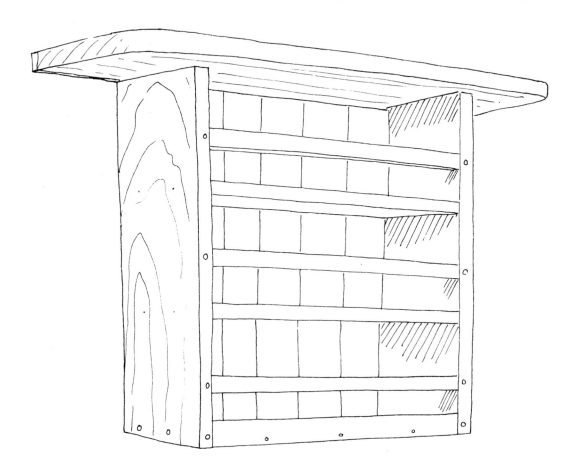

Fuming is not pleasant, though the results are often exciting. Most woods can be fumed, but woods such as oak which naturally contain tannic acid will not need the preliminary wash with acid.

You can make a fuming bag from clear polythene sheeting. Join the sides with brown parcel tape or masking tape, and arrange it so that one end can be opened easily. Ammonia in water can be bought from the cabinet-maker's suppliers listed at the back of the book. The gas which is released from the water irritates the eyes and makes breathing very painful, so take care when you handle the ammonia.

Tannic acid can be bought from many chemists, and you should dissolve a cupful of powder in about a gallon of water. Experiment with the strength of the solution in a sample fuming bottle before brushing the tannic acid onto the rack. Clean the brush in water and leave the rack to dry.

Cover the rack with the bag and place a couple of half empty cups of ammonia inside. Put one cup on the floor and the other on one of the upper shelves. Seal the bag with tape, and whenever you open the bag, hold your breath. The ammonia gas is harmful and you should not inhale it or allow it to come in contact with unprotected skin. When the rack has darkened suitably, remove it from the bag, and leave it where it can air.

Stain the rack with English Light Oak, warmed with a dash of American Walnut and Canadian Cedar. Finish by brushing the rack with three or four coats of shellac button polish, leaving each coat for about 30 minutes to dry. Instructions for brushing shellac are included on pages 101–3. Leave the rack to dry in a warm room then rub it down with 000 wire wool and apply a liberal coat of black wax polish.

Welsh Kitchen Dresser

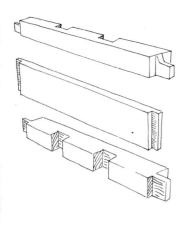

THIS TRADITIONAL English dresser (see photograph following page 96) is 4ft 9in long (1.45m) and 6ft 6in (2m) high. The dresser base is 18in (0.46m) deep. A potboard of closely fitted planks extends along the length of the base, and three deep drawers give additional useful storage space.

The frieze, extending the full length of the dresser, is cut from a single plank, recessed into the front face of the inner legs, and tenoned at the sides. Two other rails reach the full length of the base. Like the frieze, they are tenoned into the corner legs, and cross-halved with the inner legs. Although all the joint measurements are the same, the halving joints are arranged differently: seen from the front, the top rail has precedence over the inner legs, and the inner legs have precedence over the potboard rail.

The sides of the plate rack are dovetailed into the top plank, and terminate in square-sectioned feet. The shelves are held in shallow grooves cut in the sides of the rack, and a simple moulding decorates their front edges. Capping pieces with the same moulding are nailed to the front edges of the sides. The sloping cornice is made from a flat plank, mitred at the corners, and glued and nailed to the top of the rack.

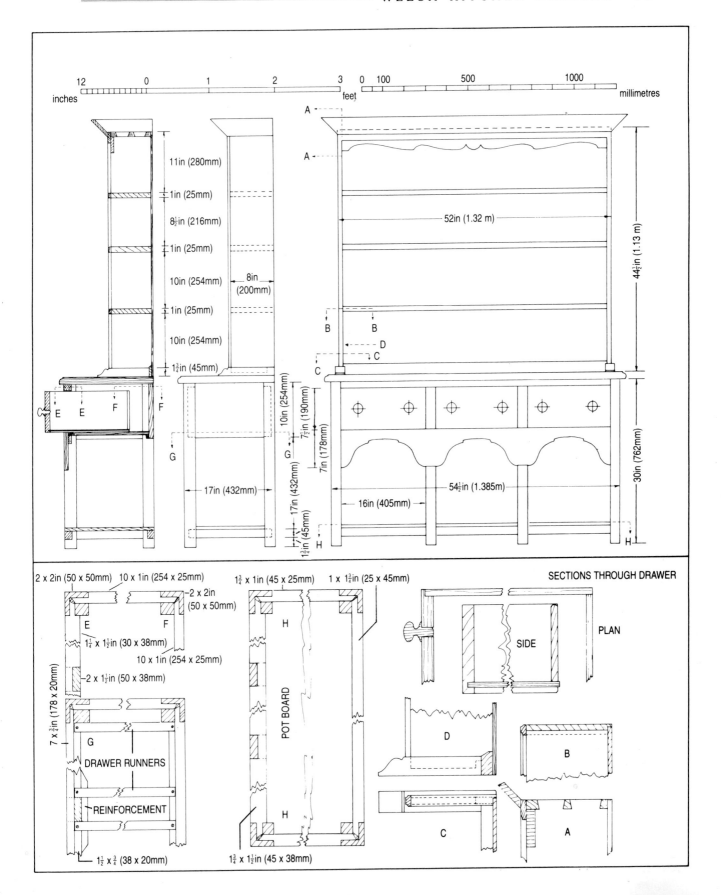

inches

12   0   1   2   3   feet

0 100   500   1000   millimetres

A

A

11in (280mm)

1in (25mm)

8½in (216mm)

1in (25mm)

10in (254mm)   8in (200mm)

1in (25mm)

10in (254mm)

1¾in (45mm)

52in (1.32 m)

44½in (1.13 m)

B   B   D   C

C

30in (762mm)

E   E   F   F

G   G

10in (254mm)   7½in (190mm)   7in (178mm)

17in (432mm)   17in (432mm)   1½in (45mm)

54½in (1.385m)

16in (405mm)

H   H

2 x 2in (50 x 50mm)   10 x 1in (254 x 25mm)

1¾ x 1in (45 x 25mm)   1 x 1¾in (25 x 45mm)

SECTIONS THROUGH DRAWER

E   F   2 x 2in (50 x 50mm)

1¼ x 1½in (30 x 38mm)

10 x 1in (254 x 25mm)

2 x 1½in (50 x 38mm)

PLAN

SIDE

7 x ¾in (178 x 20mm)

G

DRAWER RUNNERS

REINFORCEMENT

POT BOARD

H

H

D

B

C

A

1½ x ¾ (38 x 20mm)

1¾ x 1½in (45 x 38mm)

CONSTRUCTION

The legs

Cut out the four front legs. The outer legs are 2in (50mm) square, and the inner legs are 2in x 1½in (50mm x 38mm). Cut the legs to the same length, and plane them square. Hold them all together and mark the top and bottom lines for the mortices and cross-halving joints, as illustrated.

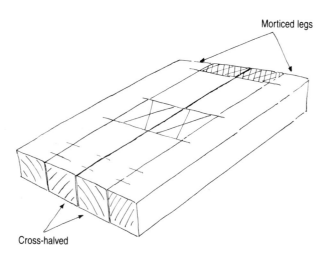

Morticed legs

Cross-halved

Morticing

Take the two corner legs, and use a marking gauge to scribe the sides of each mortice for the front framework. The long mortice for the frieze is 1in (25mm) deep, and is set back from the front face by ½in (12mm). A reinforcement rail is glued to the back of the frieze, and this butts against the inside legs.

Rout out all the mortices in the corner legs, using the router box (described on page 15), with a ⅜in (9mm) straight-sided two-flute cutter set in the router. Advice on morticing with the router box can be found on page 15.

Cross-halving

Mark and cut out the cross-halving joints in the inner legs. Joints are cut into both the front and back faces of the legs, as illustrated. The halving joints, however, should all be the same depth (¾in/20mm): equivalent to half the thickness of the leg.

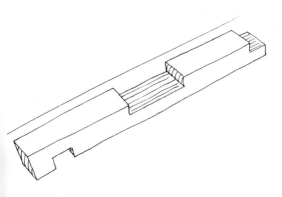

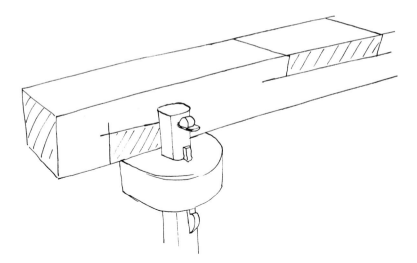

Mark the ends of each joint with a knife and set-square, and scribe the bottom of each recess with a marking gauge. Use a chisel to relieve the cutting lines at the top and bottom of each joint (see page 140). Lodge the blade of the tenon saw against the shoulder-line and saw down each side of the joint, stopping at the marking gauge. Then chisel out the waste from between the sawcuts. When you are trimming the long recess which holds the frieze, make regular cuts across the waste to make its removal easier. Chisel down close to the line, but do not chisel beyond the line.

Skimming the faces of the joints to make them level can be left until all the front legs and rails have been brought to the same stage.

The rails

Now plane the front rails square. Pencil in the face side and face edge marks, then lay the two rails together, with their ends aligned and their face sides touching. Mark the shoulders for the tenons at each end, and mark the sides of the cross-halving joints. Separate the two rails. On each halving joint, use a pencil to mark the area from which the waste has to be removed. Now incise the sides of the halving joints, using the knife only where sawcuts will be made. Do not square right around the rails, or the incisions will show up on the face side and spoil the appearance. Remember that the configuration of cross-halving joints in the two rails is different. Cut the waste from the front face of the potboard rail at its joints with the inner legs. Cut the waste from the inside face of the top rail where it cross-halves with the top end of the two inner legs.

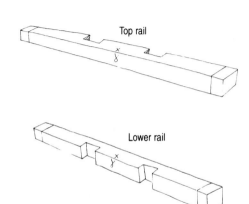

Top rail

Lower rail

Use a sharp chisel to relieve the shoulder-lines before sawing the shoulders of the tenons and the sides of the cross-halving joints. Tenon faces and the chiselled surfaces of the halving joints can now be levelled. Use the router mounted in the pillar drill stand, and set it to the exact gauge marks of the tenons and halving joints.

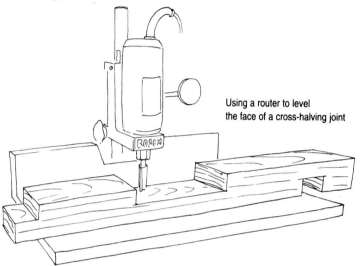

Using a router to level
the face of a cross-halving joint

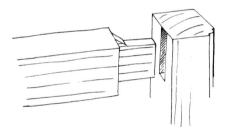

Test all the halving joints in turn, trimming each one with a chisel until they fit tightly, with their face sides level. Next saw the sloping haunches in the tenons of the top rail, and chisel the matching slope at the top of the corner leg mortices (see page 34 for advice on cutting and fitting mortice and tenon joints). Fit the tenons into the legs, then fit the tenons of the lower rail, and assemble the front framework.

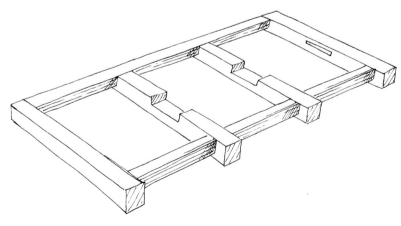

The frieze

The frieze is cut from a single plank. This is tenoned into the corner legs, and slotted into the recesses routed in the front faces of the two inner legs. When the outer legs and rails of the front framework are assembled, lay the assembly face-up on a flat surface and check that it is square by measuring the diagonals. Now, to find out whether the tops of the recesses holding the frieze plank are in line, plane one edge of the frieze plank straight and press it into the recesses in the inner legs. Nudge it upwards against the shoulders of the recesses. This will show whether the top edges of the recesses line up. They should be in line. If they are not, adjust them carefully with a chisel (after marking with a set-square and knife), until they are.

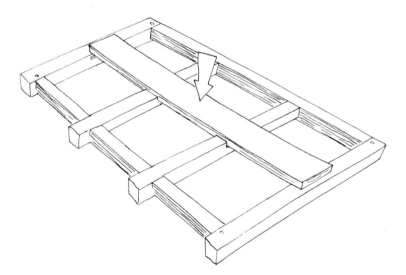

You will want the frieze plank to be a tight, neat fit, so, with the plank in position and with its top edge lined up with the top of the recesses in the inner legs, measure each slot in turn, and transfer that mark to the front face of the board. It does not matter if the board widths vary slightly, as long as the top edge is straight, and the lower joints are a close fit.

Without straying beyond these marks, plane the lower edge of the plank. Now hold the plank in position, and use a knife or chisel to mark the position of the shoulder-lines for the tenons at the ends, taking the exact positions for the marks from the edges of the outer legs, as illustrated. Square around the ends of the frieze planks. If the marks do not line up with

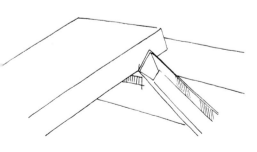

the set-square, there may be something wrong with the precision with which the framework has been laid out. Check the diagonals again with a tape measure, to find the cause of the discrepancies.

When you have satisfactory shoulder marks at each end of the frieze plank, mark off 1in (25mm) beyond the shoulder-line at each end, and cut off the waste with a tenon saw. Complete the marking out of the tenons, and then cut out the tenons in the order illustrated. First, relieve the line and saw down the shoulder, then chisel off the waste wood using a mallet and wide chisel, and finally trim the tenon with some fine paring cuts across the grain, using a chisel or rebate plane.

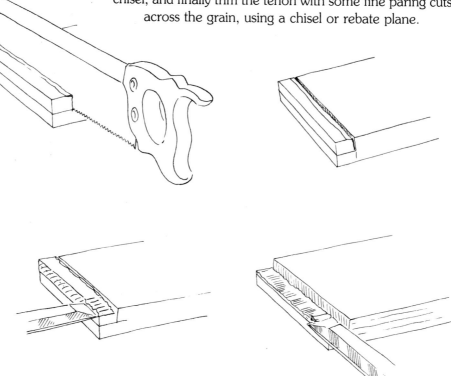

Fitting the frieze

Loosen one corner leg and fit the frieze plank. If you need to, adjust the shoulders of the joints until they all pull up tight. At this stage you can mark and cut out the frieze pattern before gluing the framework together, or you may find it easier to cut the frieze when the complete framework is fitted together. For instructions for marking and cutting the frieze see pages 62–5.

Glue the front together as soon as the joints have been fitted. Without the strength of the glue, the framework is fragile, and the cross-halving joints will work loose.

Turn the framework over, so that it lies face side down on a flat surface, protected with newspaper. In the back of each inside leg drill holes suitable for 1¼in (30mm), gauge 8 countersunk screws to hold the frieze plank and the top and bottom rails flat against the inner legs.

Each screw requires three separate drilling operations. The first is the pilot hole, which should reach to the full depth of the screw and head. The diameter of this drill should be the same as the diameter of the core of the threaded portion of the screw. The second drill should be the diameter of the upper, thicker shank, and your depth stop should be set to the length of the smooth shank plus the depth of the conical head. The third drill should be a conical countersink drill, to recess the head. If you have not got one, a larger diameter metal working drill bit will cut a suitable recess, but you must use the depth stop to prevent it cutting too quickly and deeply.

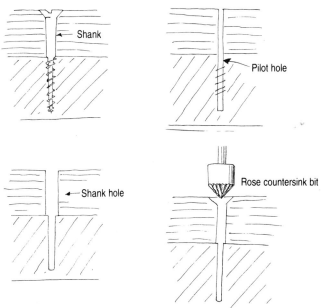

Gluing up

When this is done, glue and screw the inner legs to the frieze and the top and bottom rails, and then glue the tenons into the end legs. If the joints at the corners need pulling together, arrange short tourniquets between the inner and outer legs, as illustrated. Drill and drive in a pair of wooden pegs, and trim them flush with the legs. When the glue has dried, fit the three reinforcing battens onto which the drawer runners are glued. The battens are set parallel to the top of the frieze and about

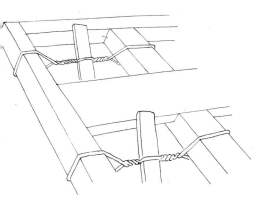

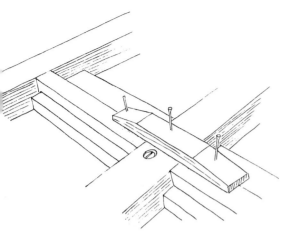

1in (25mm) (or the thickness of the drawer runners) below it. The battens butt against the legs and are glued and screwed to the frieze. Once they are fixed, glue the two tapered reinforcement pieces to link the battens.

The back framework

The back framework is constructed next. There are only two back legs, connected by a wide board at the top and a narrow rail at the bottom.

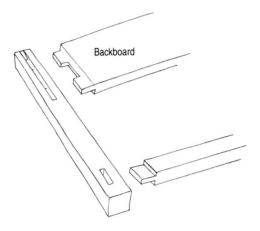

Backboard

Mark and cut out the mortices in the back legs. Notice that the side and back mortices are the same length and depth, and are offset from the outer face of the legs by similar amounts. While the router is still set up, mark and rout out the side mortices in the front, as well as the back legs.

Fit the top plank and the bottom rail which are tenoned into the back legs. The back framework should be exactly the same size as the front.

Now fit the two sides and the potboard rails into the mortices routed in the corner legs, and glue them. When the joints are clamped tight, check that the diagonals between the tops of the corner legs are identical. If they are not, pull and hold the framework square with a diagonal batten nailed between the back plank and a front leg, until the glue dries.

The potboard

The potboard is fitted next. This is made from wide planks, ⅝in–¾in (15mm–20mm) thick, nailed to the top of the lower rails. If you have two planks long enough to stretch the length of the dresser and wide enough to reach from the front to the

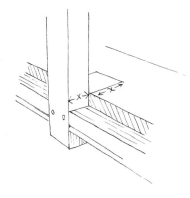

back, fit them lengthwise. Draw the positions for the legs, as illustrated, and fit the planks into position by pressing them downwards at the centre join.

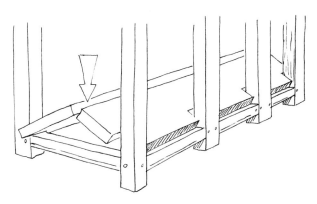

If your planking is too short or too narrow to be fitted in this way, fit the potboards at right-angles to the front of the dresser base. Fit the two end boards first, then the boards which have to be notched to fit around the inner legs. Nail these boards, and then work inwards towards the centre of each section. Do not nail them in place until they are all in position, then leave the last board a little wider than necessary.

Tape the boards more or less in place, and leave them to shrink for as long as possible, before they are nailed down.

Drawer runners

When the framework is completed, saw and fit the drawer runners and guides. These rest on the batten which reinforces the frieze, and should lie flush with the top of the frieze. Nail and glue battens to the inside face of the backboard to support the runners at the back. Fit the guides, and screw them into position, making sure that they are at right-angles to the front face of the dresser.

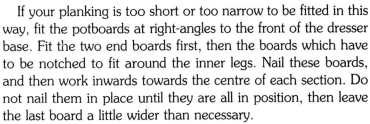

Cutting the frieze

A simple profile repeated six times, makes up the frieze. The illustration shows one section of the frieze squared with a 1in (25mm) grid which you can reproduce full size.

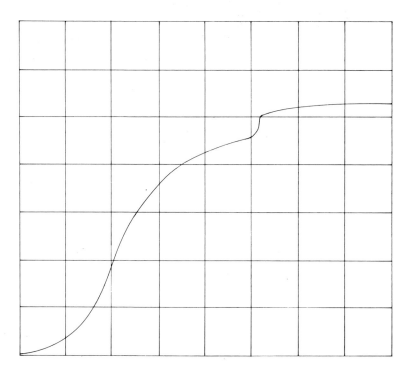

Take a piece of cardboard 12in (300mm) square and draw the 1in (25mm) grid on it. Refer to the plans, and mark the points where the frieze crosses the grid lines on the sides of each square. Pencil between the marks freehand. When you are satisfied, cut around the outline with a knife. Rest the dresser base on its back and use the template across the front of the frieze plank, flipping it at each leg to create the arches. Cut out the frieze using an electric jigsaw fitted with a T144D blade set to cut with a moderate orbital action. After sawing out the frieze, sand the edges with 90 grit paper, backed by a sanding block. Use a curved backing block to sand the concave curves.

The drawers

The dresser drawers are made from an assortment of woods. Only the drawer fronts are of oak, matching the frieze and framework, the rest is made of available offcuts, and the joints are nailed.

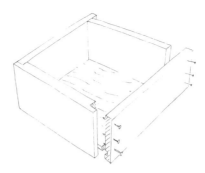

Cut and fit the drawer fronts first. Plane the blanks to width so that they fit into the drawer spaces, before trimming the ends to length. If you need to remove a fine shaving from the ends of the drawer blanks, hold them against the end stop of a simple home-made shooting board and trim the overhang with a sharp shoulder plane, used on its side (see page 143).

Drawer sides and back

Cut the sides and back planks to width. The backs are ¾in (20mm) narrower than the sides, because they sit across the bottoms of the drawer. Fit a suitable straight cutter in the router, mount the router in the router stand, and groove the bottoms of the sides and the drawer front.

Using the same straight cutter, set the fence and depth for the lap joints, check the settings on a scrap offcut, and rout out the rebate, cutting away no more than 1⁄16in (1.5mm) at a single pass. With each change of setting, make sure that all the clamping screws on the router stand are tight. If these are loose, the router will vibrate, and make machining difficult. To speed up this operation, use a vacuum cleaner to remove the cuttings, and deal with all the drawers in order, before changing the settings.

Pre-drill the sides before nailing and gluing them to the front. Trim the back plank to length, then nail it in place.

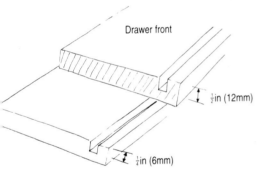

Drawer front

½in (12mm)

¼in (6mm)

Drawer bottoms

The drawer bottoms are made from thin planks of varied width, fitted and glued in situ. Plane the top sides and the edges of the drawer bottom planks. Fit the bottom planks into the inverted drawer, gluing each plank to the one you have just fitted. Do not force the drawer bottoms in place, or you will distort the sides. If you find that the drawer bottoms on the inside surface are not level, you can pin them with short panel pins, as illustrated. Drive three pins into the edge of the piece you are fitting, and cut off the pin heads, leaving ¼in (6mm) poking out of the side. Press the new panel into the grooves in the drawer sides, and hold it flush with the existing plank.

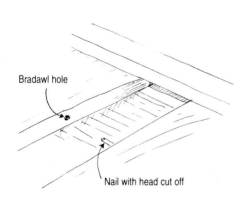

Bradawl hole

Nail with head cut off

Press the new piece so that the pins indent the edge of the first plank. Remove the new plank, and use a bradawl to deepen the indents. Glue the joint and tap the new plank into position. Glue thin runners against the sides of the drawer to increase the bearing surface.

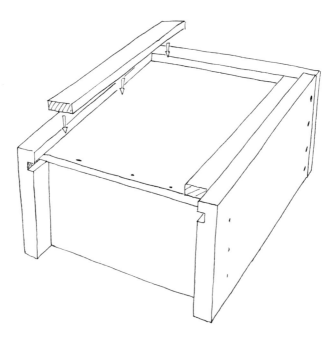

Sanding and gluing

Sand the fronts of the drawers and round their edges with a notched hardwood stick. Use the very simple moulding cutter illustrated here to indent a fine line round the edges of the drawer front.

Fit the three drawers, then glue and screw the drawer runners and the drawer stops into position.

The top

The top is made from oak planks, butt-jointed and tenoned together. Instructions for shooting, morticing and pegging the joints, and smoothing the top, can be found on page 52. Cut the ends to length after the top planks have been glued together and scraped and sanded smooth. Then rout the simple edge moulding on its upper edge, taking care to keep steady sideways pressure on the fence to prevent the cutter from digging in at the corners. Sandpaper the mouldings with 150 paper backed by a solid block, to remove traces of the router.

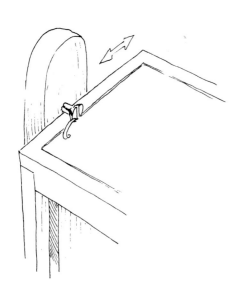

The top is pegged to the framework. In addition to the pegs, screws or glue blocks can be used to hold it securely to the front and back framework.

You will need about a dozen oak pegs, 2in (50mm) long, and a little more than ¼in (6mm) in diameter. Make the pegs in the same way as the chair pegs are made (see page 24), splitting rather than sawing them to size, and trimming them with a chisel. The pegs should be slightly tapered, and almost square at the top. Because they will be holding the top in place, it is worthwhile splitting the points of some of the pegs, and inserting a fine wedge, which will expand the peg as the wedge hits the bottom of the peg hole.

Clamp the top in position, and mark and drill the peg holes using a ¼in (6mm) brad-point drill. Make sure that the drill stop is set so that the pegs will not disappear beneath the surface of the dresser once they are driven in.

Run a little glue into each hole, then tap the pegs in place. You can now trim them flat with a sharp, bevel-edged chisel.

Sand the top of the dresser with 220 grit open cut paper. If you have not already done so, nail the loose potboards into place. If you feel a little unsure about the strength of the joint between the top of the dresser and the framework, you can turn the base upside down and fit glue blocks, 1in (25mm) square and 3in (75mm) long, around the inside of the framework, gluing them on the two touching surfaces. Chisel a chamfer on the remaining edge. Alternatively, you can pre-drill and then drive countersunk-headed screws through the rail into the top, and inside the framework at the back and sides. Gouge out the recesses as illustrated, and use these as screwing points.

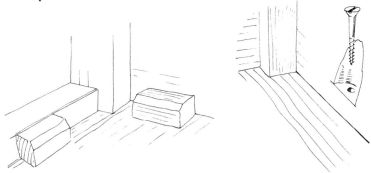

See pages 101–3 for advice on staining and polishing, and page 99 for advice on fitting handles and knobs.

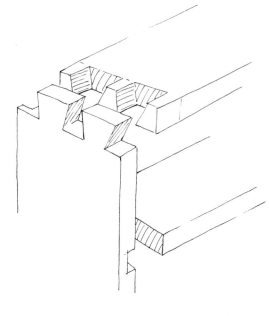

The plate rack

Like the dresser base, the plate rack is large and awkward to lift. Make some space in your workshop for the rack before you begin to assemble it.

The rack should be made of the same wood as the dresser base except for the backboards, which can be made from any available wood. If you can, use planks of differing widths; they will look more attractive than machine-finished tongue and grooving. If you prefer a rack without backboards, you can dispense with the rebates in the back edge of the sides, and you will need slightly wider planks for the shelving.

Simple through-dovetails hold the sides to the top, and the shelves are located in recesses routed in the sides. A moulded capping piece covers the edges of the sides and the shelves, and feet are tenoned onto the sides for stability.

The sides and top

Cut out the planks for the sides and the top. Plane them and mark their face sides and face edges, then clamp the two side planks in the vice, face sides together. Then mark off the shoulder-lines for the tenons at the bottom, the shelf housings, and the dovetail pins at the top.

Separate the sides and rebate them with the router. Then change the fence and depth adjustments of the router, and rout the tenons at the bottom of each side. Finish cutting out the tenon, which is inset from the back edge as illustrated.

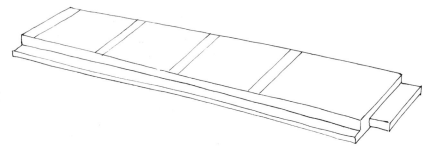

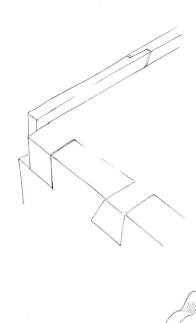

Square around the tops of the sides with a marking knife and a set-square, then pencil in the dovetail pins on the top edges of the sides. Note that the top plank is offset slightly, and lines up with the inside edge of the rebate. This allows the back planking to run onto the back of the top plank.

Cut out the dovetails, then fit the pins. Instructions for cutting these large, rather crude dovetails, and for fitting the pins, can be found on pages 112–13.

Now square across the shelf marks, and mark the bottom of the shelf groove with a marking gauge. Relieve the lines on the waste side using a chisel, then saw down the shoulder-lines of the groove with a tenon saw. Stop when you reach the gauge marks, and remove the waste with a sharp chisel.

Cut the other shelf slots in the same way. If the shelves are of uneven section, then you will have to mark them as illustrated, saw and chisel out the waste, and then trim the slot to fit.

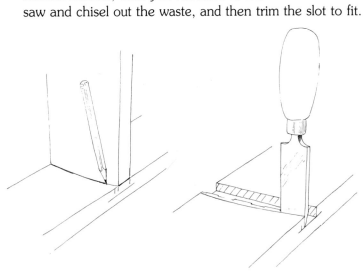

The feet

Now cut out and fit the two feet. Cut out the wide notch at the back of each foot, then mark and cut out the mortices with a ½in (12mm) two-flute router cutter. Saw the short curve at the front of the leg with a jigsaw or coping saw, and smooth it with a sharp chisel. Trim the tenons to fit into the mortices, and glue them in place.

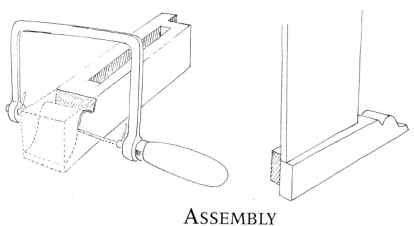

ASSEMBLY

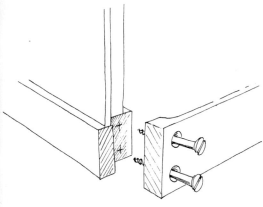

Assemble the rack. First knock the dovetails together, then slip the bottom shelf into place. Check that the framework is square, and the sides are parallel, then nail through the sides to hold the shelf in place. Fit and nail the second shelf. Fit the skirting plank between the two feet, bevel its top edge, and glue and screw it in place.

Check that the framework of the rack has remained square, and hold it square with a short diagonal batten nailed between the shelf and one side. You must also inspect the rack for another equally important distortion. Sight across the sides, as illustrated: the two sides should appear parallel. If they are not, prop the

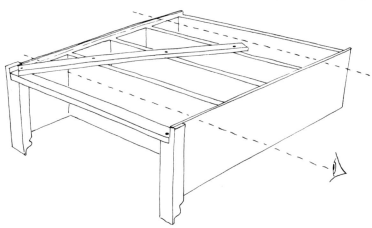

flimsy structure until they are parallel. The back will hold it stiff and straight. Fit the backboards, nailing the first board into the rebate, onto the top, and onto the shelving. Continue right across the back of the rack, removing the temporary batten when it gets in your way.

Fit the frieze plank into the top of the rack. This can either be nailed and glued into place, or lapped as illustrated. When this is fitted, design and saw out the frieze. The plans show a simple frieze, and the dresser featured in the photograph has a different one. The frieze does not need to match or reflect the frieze on the dresser base; a geometrical pattern would be suitable, or you could design a curved, pierced frieze terminating in the centre with a spoked wheel. There are any number of options available, and if you look in antiques guides or country house magazines you will be sure to find some inspiration.

The illustration shows a moulding which you can make easily, and use to cover the front edges of the shelves and sides. Cut and plane sufficient regular-sectioned stock to cap the sides and fronts of the shelves, and a wider piece to cover the top. The simple moulding is cut with a router, fitted with a radius cutter. Arrange a firm fence and a sprung stick to hold the workpiece against the fence as the work is passed across the router. Rout all the mouldings. You will have to cut the moulding in two stages, so lower the cutter to full depth when all the mouldings have had their first pass.

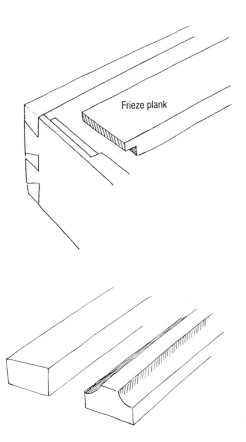

Frieze plank

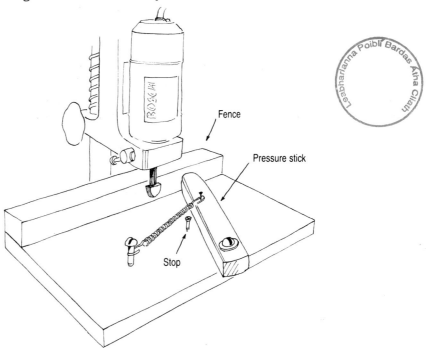

Fence

Pressure stick

Stop

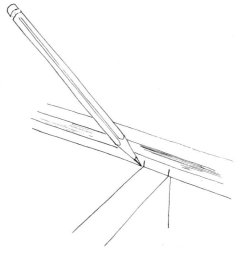

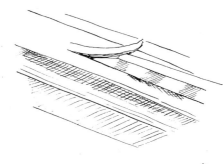

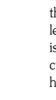

Front

Returns

Capping the edges

Sand the mouldings using a short length of dowel wrapped in 90 grit sandpaper. Glue and nail the top capping piece to the top of the frieze plank, and then fit the side pieces. When they are cut to length and lodge tightly between the top piece and the feet at each side, mark on the positions for the shelf caps. They are fitted with a simple mitred joint as shown, and are chiselled out once a sawcut has been made at each side of the joint, as illustrated.

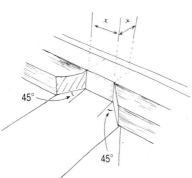

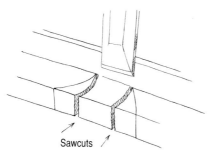

Sawcuts

The capping pieces are nailed and glued to the sides. You can punch the nails below the surface of the cap and fill the hole, or you can conceal the nail by first lifting a splinter of the capping piece with a ⅛in (4mm) chisel, driving in the nail and then gluing back the splinter. Hold the splinter with masking tape while the glue dries. After sanding, it will be almost impossible to spot the nail. Once the side pieces are fitted, shape and fit the shelf caps. These are first cut to length, and then the mitres are shaved to a close fit, using a chisel. Nail and glue these in place, and sand them smooth and level when the glue has dried.

The cornice

The cornice is made from a thin plank of oak. The plank should be at least 7ft (2.15m) long, to allow for the mitres which will have to be cut from it. Set your angle bevel to the angle at which the cornice slopes from the face of the rack, and plane the lower edge to that angle. Do not cut the cornice plank to length: the mitre joints at the corners take a lot of wood, and it is best to work from one end of a long plank, rather than to risk cutting the sections roughly to length first and then find you have made a mistake.

Opposite: **Spanish Chair, page 8**

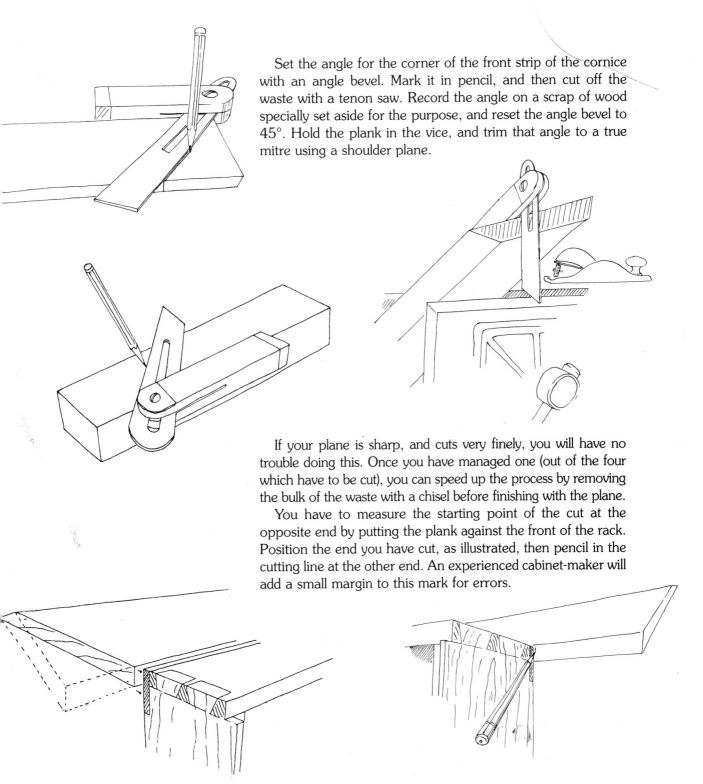

Set the angle for the corner of the front strip of the cornice with an angle bevel. Mark it in pencil, and then cut off the waste with a tenon saw. Record the angle on a scrap of wood specially set aside for the purpose, and reset the angle bevel to 45°. Hold the plank in the vice, and trim that angle to a true mitre using a shoulder plane.

If your plane is sharp, and cuts very finely, you will have no trouble doing this. Once you have managed one (out of the four which have to be cut), you can speed up the process by removing the bulk of the waste with a chisel before finishing with the plane.

You have to measure the starting point of the cut at the opposite end by putting the plank against the front of the rack. Position the end you have cut, as illustrated, then pencil in the cutting line at the other end. An experienced cabinet-maker will add a small margin to this mark for errors.

Opposite: **Lakeland Armchair, page 126**

Ask for some help, or tack the cornice in its exact position at the first end, before marking the second. When you have marked the corner of the rack on the inside face of the cornice, reset your angle bevel to the angle at which the sawcut was made at the first end, and mark this line on the outside face of the cornice. Check this very carefully before sawing. The mitre that you are cutting extends much further than you might think, and you must make sure that you have made adequate allowance for this. Add a little extra in case of errors, and then saw the second cut. Trim the new sawcut, and nail and glue the front part of the cornice in position.

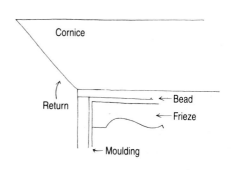

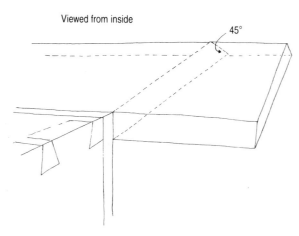

Viewed from inside

45°

Gluing

The return mitres on the cornice are cut in the same way, and they are trimmed to fit against the front plank. Glue and nail the returns to the sides of the rack, tape across the mitre joints, then support them with glue blocks slipped into each mitre joint, and into the triangle formed at the back of the return, between the side of the dresser and the cornice. Finally, cut the returns to length. Sand the face of the cornice, but do not round off the mitre, which should remain hard and sharp.

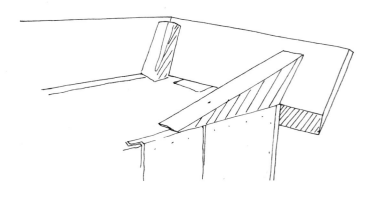

Fitting the handles

The addresses of suppliers who stock reproduction brassware can be found at the back of the book. The handles come ready for insertion in the drawer front, and are held in position with a nut and bolt.

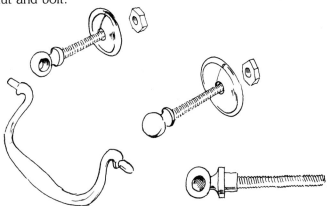

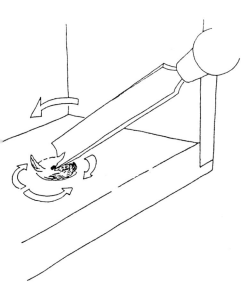

Mark the position of the handles very carefully before drilling the bolt holes with a ³⁄₁₆in (5mm) drill. On some fittings, the brass cups holding the handle have a shoulder, and a slightly larger drill will have to be used to enlarge the hole and allow the cup to clamp the decorative plate successfully. Sometimes you might find that the bolt threaded into the inside of the cup is too short, and cannot be fitted with the nut. If this is the case, gouge a recess on the inside of the drawer front, as illustrated. Once you have tested that the drawer handles fit, remove them, and wait until the dresser is finished before fitting them.

FINISHING

This dresser has been stained and shellac polished. It has a brushed shellac finish, which has been waxed with a generous application of black, quick-drying wax.

Preparation

Arrange a strong light to illuminate your work. A halogen workshop floodlight is ideal. When you are preparing and finishing the dresser you must work in a bright light, set a little above head height and positioned slightly to one side of where you are working.

You will have to separate the two parts of the dresser, and unless you have a large workshop, you may have to finish them separately. If you do, make certain that you mix enough stain so that the whole job can be finished with the same colour. It is very difficult to match a colour once it has been applied to a piece of wood.

Inspect the dresser carefully. This is the moment to try to hide faulty workmanship by filling cracks and overlong mortices with wood filler. But before you start, bear in mind that country furniture need not be technically perfect. In some of the most beautiful old furniture there are bad joints, cracks and signs of hurried workmanship. When the wood is stained a darker colour, the blemishes may not be so obvious, they might even be filled with furniture wax. However, if you fill them, you must consider the difficulty of staining fillers, many of which do not absorb stain at all, and the additional difficulty of cleaning away excess filler, which often anchors itself to the wood close to the blemish, repels the stain and draws unwelcome attention to the area.

If you are in doubt, punch the nail heads below the wood surface, and fill them with a two-part wood filler of a suitable tone and colour. Colour is less important than tone, but your filler should be at least as dark as the wood which will surround it. Fill cracks in the cornice mitre joints, and between the cornice moulding and the front face of the dresser. Try to avoid filling anywhere else. Mix and apply the filler according to the instructions supplied with it. Give the filler ample time to harden, and then slice away any surplus with a sharp chisel held flat against the surface of the wood. Finish sanding the filler with 150 grit garnet paper, backed by a foam block, in the direction of the grain.

Sanding

Sand the mouldings and cornices with 220 grit paper, backed by suitably curved blocks, or with small sheets of fine cut steel sandplate, glued to small blocks of wood. When the awkward areas have been sanded, and there are no machining marks visible on the mouldings, sandpaper the remainder of the dresser and rack. To expedite matters, use 220 grit open cut paper in an orbital sander, and apply minimum hand pressure. Inspect the paper regularly, and renew it as soon as it tears or clogs. When using an orbital sander you must wear a face mask.

Staining

Vacuum or brush the dust from the dresser, cut some clean dry cotton rags into squares for staining, and collect some offcuts of the wood you have used to do some staining tests. Note that the grain of the timber will affect the take-up of the stain. Areas close to knots and end-grain will absorb far more colour than other parts of a plank, so it may be necessary for you to mix two tints of stain, one slightly more dilute to be used on the end-grain and rougher woods.

The oak dresser illustrated was coloured with a mixture of American Walnut, Canadian Cedar, and English Light Oak. To make up a lighter stain for the end-grain, dilute the colour with English Light Oak. Work on one face of the dresser at a time. Arrange suitable lighting, then lift one end of the dresser onto a trestle, and stain it. Start in an inconspicuous place, just in case you do not like the colour, but always make sure that you have enough stain mixed, because you do not want to run out of stain before you have finished.

First make sure there is good ventilation, then put on rubber gloves and begin to apply the stain liberally, either with a brush, or with a rag bundled into a neat wad. Apply the stain in the direction of the grain, trying to keep a wet edge at all times. As you apply the colour with one hand, use a clean rag in the other hand to even out the application, pushing the stain into parts that have been missed, and wiping away puddles.

Once you have stained the dresser base, sides and cornice of the rack, you can stain the awkward places such as the pot-board, the planks at the back of the rack, the underside of the top and the shelves of the rack, using a wide brush. Wipe away runs and puddles with a rag. Before the stain dries, inspect the dresser closely, and touch in any areas you have missed. Then tilt the dresser back and stain the feet. Stain the drawers on the top edge and sides, as well as the fronts.

Leave the stain to dry for about 30 minutes, then brush slightly thinned button (orange coloured) or garnet (dark brown coloured) shellac polish onto the dresser.

Use a 3in (75mm) wide, good quality paint brush for applying the shellac polish. Decant two or three cupfuls of shellac into a plastic freezer tub, and add a small splash of methylated spirits or finishing spirits.

Shellac is applied very quickly in thin coats. You will need to replenish the brush frequently, and you will find that it is almost impossible to brush an even finish. Always apply the shellac in

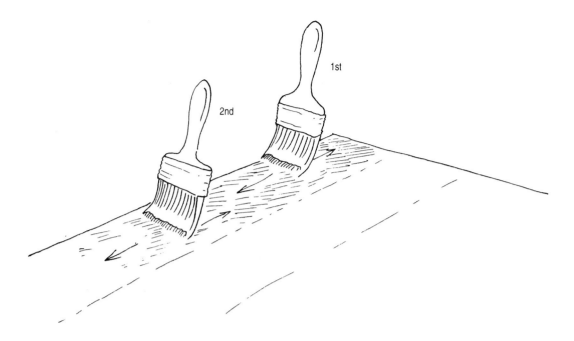

the direction of the grain. Dip the tip of the brush into the shellac, press it against the side of the tub to remove the excess,
and then brush the shellac quickly onto the side of the dresser,
brushing up and down the grain away from where you started.
The first brush load should reach the edge and end of the plank
and extend a few inches in the other direction. The second
application starts a short distance further down the plank from
where you ran out, and works back, and then on a little further.
Do not worry too much about evenness, because after four or
five coats the surface will need to be rubbed down with fine
wire wool anyway, and that will hide the worst problems.

Apply three coats to the sides of the dresser, four to the
front, potboard and cornice, and five coats to the dresser base
top. The backboards and shelves of the rack will probably need
three coats. The capping pieces will need four, because they
will attract attention and need to be silky smooth. The same is
true of the drawer fronts and the frieze.

When you have finished with the shellac, wash the brush in
methylated spirits, and pour the shellac back into its container.
Leave the dresser to dry. You should leave it for at least 4 hours
in a warm room, and overnight if you can, so the shellac
becomes quite hard.

Now take a wad of 0000 or 000 wire wool, bunch it in your
hand and rub the sides of the dresser. Rub lightly in the direction of the grain. The wire wool will remove the glitter from the
surface and leave it with a satin, rather dusty finish. Tap the
wire wool regularly to prevent it clogging with shellac dust, and

replace it when it has lost its edge. Rub all the polished surfaces of the dresser and rack. If you think that some parts need more polish, vacuum off the dust, and continue with your applications. At this point you can change the colour of the polish by adding spirit soluble Red Mahogany aniline dye to the garnet, or some Oak or Walnut to the button polish. (Dissolve the dye in meths or finishing spirit and strain it, before stirring it into the polish.)

After the dresser has been rubbed down, fit the handles. When you have done this, you can either wax polish the dresser and rack with a quick-drying, black wax polish, or you can try a little faking and ageing, using dry powder colours mixed with PVA woodworker's white glue. Make up a dark brown paste of glue and colour, and dab it on with a brush. You can use it to colour bad filling, or to even up an area of uneven staining. You may want to paint some dirt marks onto the drawer fronts below the handles. Dab the wet paint with a damp rag to remove the brush marks. These paint marks will dry white, but the subsequent coat of wax will obliterate the white. If you do not like what you have done, the marks can be removed with a warm, damp rag.

Wear rubber gloves when you are wax polishing. Apply the wax plentifully with a rag, heavily dipped in the moist wax. Rub it over a small area of wood, then immediately wipe it off with a large, clean piece of rag. Allow wax to accumulate in crevices and tight corners. After the wax has had a short while to dry, burnish it with a lambswool mop, mounted in an electric drill.

IRISH PINE SETTLE

THIS IS A SMALL settle with room for two people to sit comfortably. The back planking reaches from the headrest to the floor, but the angle of the planking is broken at seat level, where the lower planks flare back to form a skirt. There are no joints apart from the simple notches in the sides that hold the three cross supports, and the lap joints between the back planking.

It takes a lot of wood to make a settle; the settle shown in the photograph following page 96 is made from larch, purchased rough-sawn. My friend Annemarie's antique settle, of which this is a copy, is made from Baltic pine. Almost any wood will do, but it should be well seasoned and dry, because with plank widths of 12in (300mm) or more there can be considerable shrinkage.

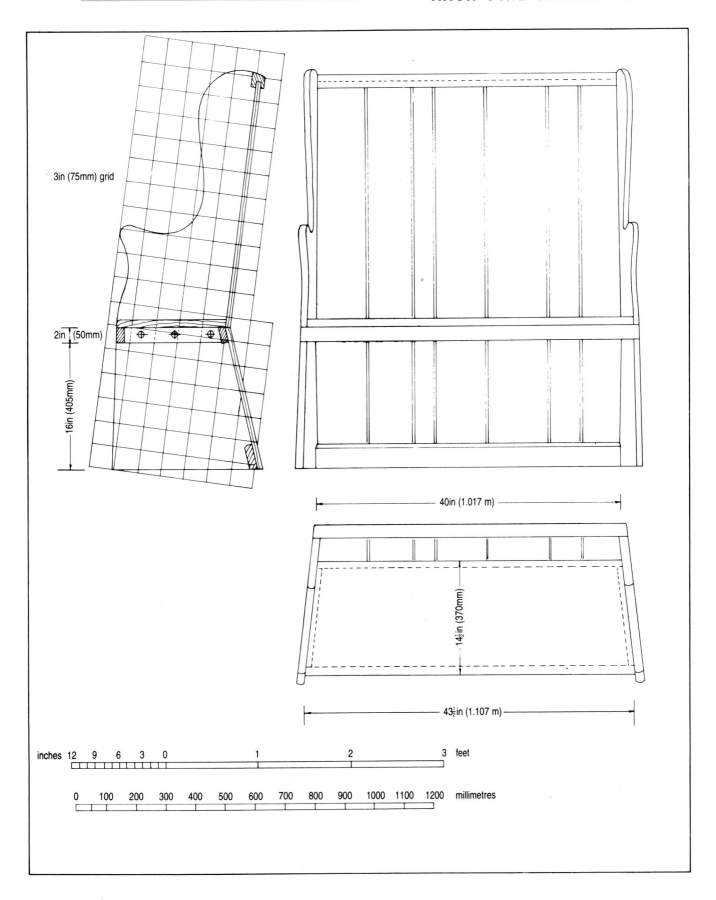

3in (75mm) grid

2in (50mm)

16in (405mm)

40in (1.017 m)

14½in (370mm)

43½in (1.107 m)

inches 12   9   6   3   0   1   2   3   feet

0   100   200   300   400   500   600   700   800   900   1000 1100 1200   millimetres

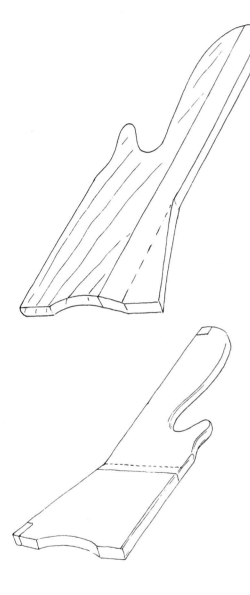

CONSTRUCTION

The sides

Use the squared grid drawn on the plan to reproduce a full-sized cardboard template of one side of the settle. Lay the template on one of the 1in (25mm) thick side planks, and draw around it. Plank widths will vary, so try to arrange the template so the curved front edge of the settle is cut from a single piece. Additional slabs can be butt-jointed to the back edge to make the width.

When both ends are marked, saw them out with a jigsaw, and make up the extra width at the backs with the offcuts. Plane the joining faces square and straight, and glue them together, then trim the ends to their exact shape. Sand the inside and outside faces of the sides, using 150 then 220 grit paper mounted in an orbital sander. Round the front edges with a chisel and sand them with 220 grit paper. These edges do not need to be perfectly rounded, and will look better if they are left with the chisel marks still visible, except where people will be expected to hold or rub against the wood.

Clamp the two sides together, and using the template for reference, mark the top lines for the seat support on the front edges, and the lines for the top rail and skirting board at the back. Separate the pieces, and pencil in the line marking the underside of the seat on each inside face, using the template for reference.

The illustration shows that the bearing faces of the notches cut in the splayed sides will be bevelled. The angles can be marked and measured before assembly, but it is important to remember that the depth gauge can be used on only one side of a side for each notch: on the outside face for the seat support at the front, and the inside face for the back crosspieces.

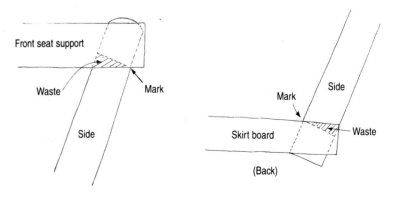

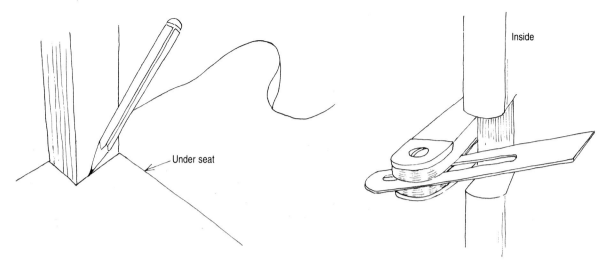

Hold the front seat support, as illustrated, and mark round it. Relieve the shoulder-lines, then saw down each one. Remove the waste between the sawcuts with a jigsaw, and chisel the edge to the required bevel, using an angle bevel set to the appropriate angle for reference. Fit the support, and repeat at the other end. Cut and fit the other notches.

Now fit the two wooden cleats to the inside faces of the sides, as illustrated. Note that the cuts at the ends are bevelled to match the sides. Glue and nail them in place.

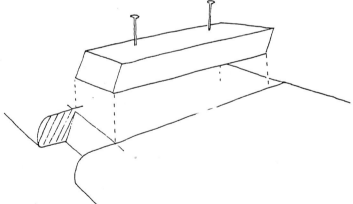

The seat

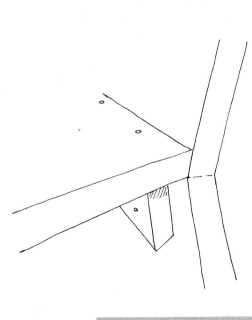

Cut out the seat plank, rounding the top edge of the front, and angling the sides inwards towards the back. Plane the back edge of the seat to line up with the slope of the back. The back planking is nailed to the back edge of the seat, so the joint between them will be visible from the front. The seat plank fits against the sides on top of the battens, and on the seat support at the front. Fit the ends and the seat together. A G-cramp at each end should hold them together while you make a note of any additional trimming needed to the slots of the seat supports.

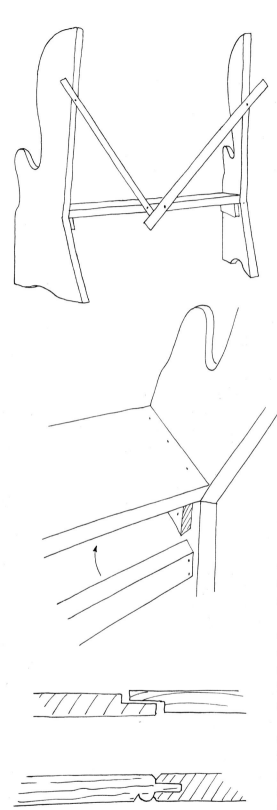

ASSEMBLY

Dismantle the pieces, adjust the slots, and then reassemble them. Glue the seat support into its slots, and nail and glue the seat in position. Tack some diagonal battens from the back of the seat to the sides, to hold them vertical while the glue dries.

When the glue has dried, fit the bevelled support under the seat; its ends should be trimmed to suit the angles at the sides. Plane the top edge to tilt the support level with the flared sides of the lower back. When this is done, glue and nail the support in position.

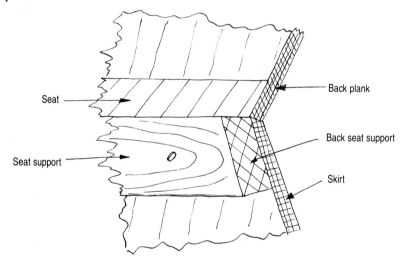

Cut, groove and fit the top rail into the notches in the back edge, and glue and screw it in position. Fit and glue the lower skirting rail, holding it in position at the ends with countersunk steel screws.

The back planking is arranged in two sections. The lower end of the upper planks is sawn square and nailed to the back of the seat, butted against the lower planks. As the plans show, the top edges of the skirt planking is bevelled to fit tight against the lower edge of the top planks, and it is nailed to the seat support.

The back planks can either be tongue and grooved together, or lapped. A small bead can be worked on the shoulder of the tongue, as illustrated. The tongues and grooves are cut with a router, and the bead can either be scraped using a scratch stock, or machined with a corner bead cutter mounted in the router.

Fit the top planks first. Sand each plank before trimming it to length. Allow plenty of overhang at the sides, as each tongue will reduce the width of the planks by about ½in (12mm). Cut the planks to length, with accurate square cuts at each end. Next, rout out all the tongues, using an arbor cutter, then scrape or rout the small bead moulding on the shoulder of the tongue.

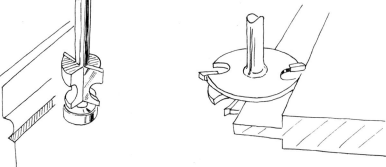

Change the arbor setting, and rout out the grooves on the edges opposite to the tongues. Leave one plank without a groove. The edge of this one will be nailed to the side of the settle.

Now fit the planking. Bevel the side of the first plank. This plank is nailed to the edge of the settle, and to the back of the seat. Make sure that each plank rests against the top rail when fitted without nudging the top rail upwards. Pin the top edge of the plank into the top rail before continuing with the next plank. Trim the last plank to width before nailing it. Plane it flush once the edge has been nailed.

Fit the planks at the bottom of the seat. Work across the seat in the same way as before, bevelling the top edge. If possible, try to match the planks, so that the tongue and groove appears to continue right down the back of the settle. Nail the bottoms of the planks to the skirting board at floor level.

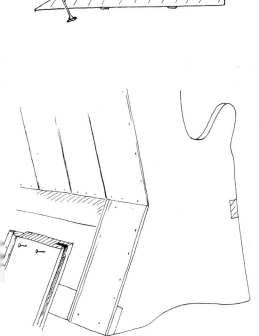

FINISHING

Sand the settle and prepare it for finishing. The settle in the photograph has been finished with three applications of wax polish, which is a finish that will improve with use. If your settle is made from pine, either wax in the same way, or use the finishing schedule of stain and button polish applied to the Normandy cupboard (see page 125).

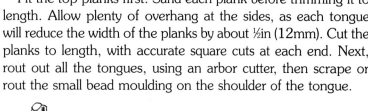

NORMANDY CUPBOARD

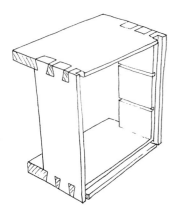

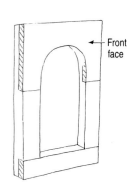

Front face

THIS IS A SMALL cupboard, little more than 16in (400mm) square, but large enough to hold eight or ten cups, and several small porringers and children's drinking cups (see photograph following page 96). It can be hung on a wall, or perched at the back of a work surface.

The carcass of the cupboard is dovetailed together, and the back is recessed in a shallow rebate. Two shelves slide into grooves cut in the sides, the upper shelf has a rail fitted to its front edge.

The framework of each door is cross-halved together, the horizontal rails crossing in front of the vertical stiles. This arrangement enables an arch to be cut at the top without leaving an area of weak and fragile end-grain at the sides.

The pillars, blocks and beads are cut from solid wood, and glued onto the fronts of the doors. From the plans, you can see that the pillars and beads are not turned on a lathe, but are shaped by hand plane and smoothed with sandpaper. The cornice moulding and the moulding at the bottom of the cupboard are cut with a router.

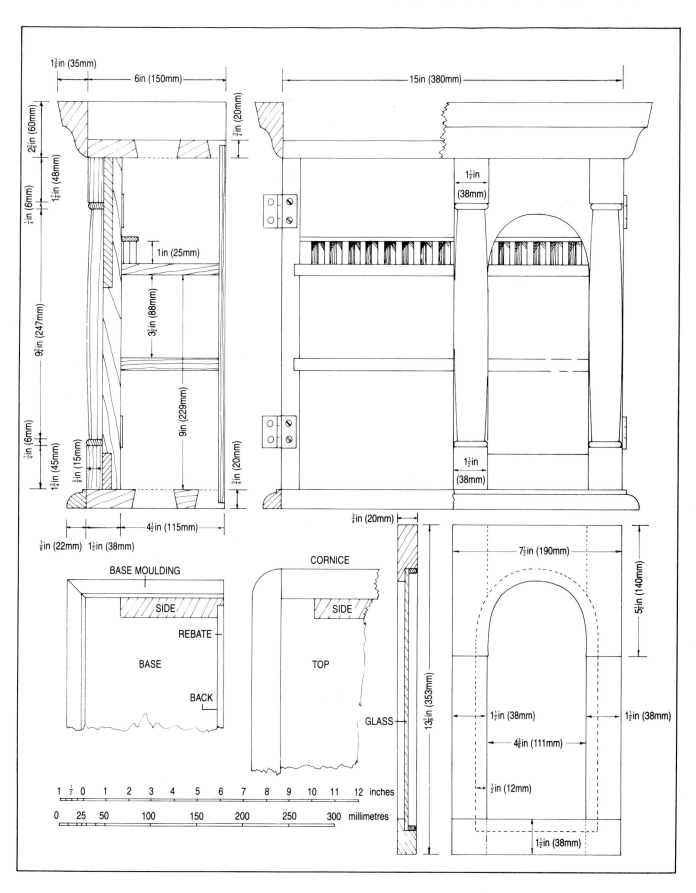

1⅜in (35mm)

6in (150mm)

15in (380mm)

¾in (20mm)

2⅜in (60mm)

1⅞in (48mm)

¼in (6mm)

1½in (38mm)

1in (25mm)

3½in (88mm)

9¼in (247mm)

9in (229mm)

¼in (6mm)

1¾in (45mm)

⅝in (15mm)

1½in (38mm)

¾in (20mm)

4½in (115mm)

⅞in (22mm)   1½in (38mm)

BASE MOULDING

SIDE

REBATE

BASE

BACK

CORNICE

SIDE

TOP

GLASS

¾in (20mm)

13⅞in (353mm)

7½in (190mm)

5½in (140mm)

1½in (38mm)

1½in (38mm)

4⅜in (111mm)

½in (12mm)

1½in (38mm)

1 ½ 0   1   2   3   4   5   6   7   8   9   10   11   12   inches

0   25   50   100   150   200   250   300   millimetres

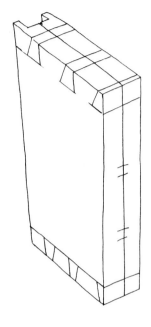

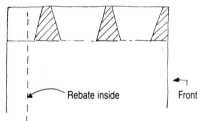

Rebate inside   Front

CONSTRUCTION

This cupboard is made from cheap spruce planks, with chestnut mouldings and decorations, and elm shelves. The back is made from a small sheet of Medium Density Fibreboard (MDF), stained brown.

The carcass

Make the carcass of the cupboard first. The sides, top and bottom are made from ¾in (20mm) thick planking. The side planks are sawn 4⅜in (111mm) wide, and the top plank and bottom planks are 6in (150mm) wide. Use the router to cut the rebates in the back edges of all four planks. Instructions for rebating with the router can be found on page 149. Then cut the planks to length, and clamp the pairs together, so the shoulders can be marked in.

The dovetails

Square round the shoulders with a set-square and knife and then pencil in and cut the dovetails. These should be drawn freehand, and arranged as illustrated. (For advice on cutting out through-dovetails see page 50.)

Saw down the sides of the tails, and remove the waste between the two tails with a coping saw. Chop out the remaining waste with a ⅝in (15mm) bevel-edged chisel and mallet, working first from the outside to the centre of the plank, and then from the inside.

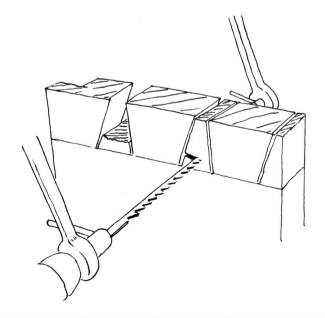

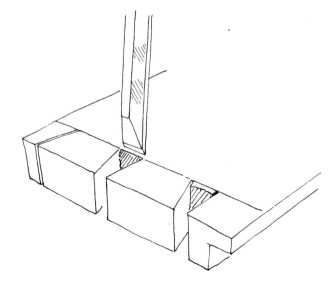

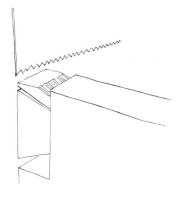

Relieve the lines at the edges of the boards and saw off the waste at the corners, as illustrated. Trim any waste that may remain proud of the shoulder-line. If you have allowed the saw to wander below the shoulder-line, the blemish is unlikely to show when the cupboard is finished. Repeat at the other ends of the sides.

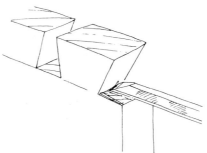

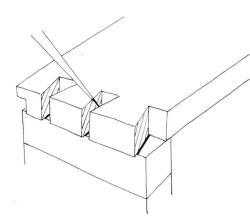

Now mark the pins by aligning the side over the top, which is held vertically in the vice, and scribing the sides of the tails onto the end-grain of the top. To ensure a tight fit, remember to move the tails a short distance in the direction of the arrow (see page 50). This effectively widens the pins, and enables you to saw down the centre of each scribe line to the shoulder-lines without worrying that the pins will be loose.

Once the pins are marked and sawn on the end of the top, lift the top by about 2in–3in (50mm–75mm) in the vice, and saw out the waste between the pins with the coping saw. Chisel the waste back to the shoulder-line as illustrated.

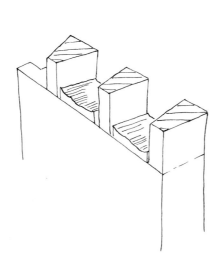

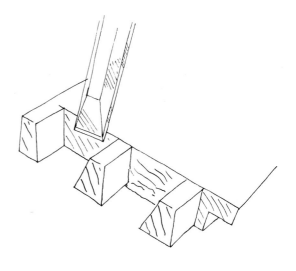

Fit the first dovetails, adjust them as necessary, and then cut and fit the pins at the other end of the top. Remember to line up the back edges when you are scribing the joints. The top, which is wider than the rest, will overhang the front, but the backs must all be level.

Shelf grooves

When all four joints are complete, separate the sides, and after aligning and clamping them together, mark the positions for the two shelf grooves. Separate the pieces and square across the sides with a set-square, then mark the depth of the groove at the front edge with a marking gauge.

Relieve the lines and saw the sides of the grooves with a tenon saw (see page 140), then chisel out the waste from between the sawcuts.

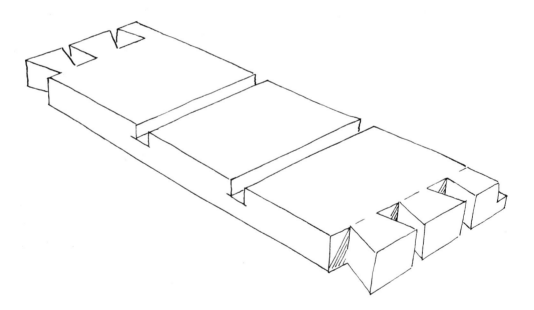

When all four grooves have been cut, assemble the four sides. Cut a piece of plywood or MDF board to fit into the rebate at the back, and trim it to fit. Now, dismantle the carcass, glue the joints, and reassemble it, driving a 1½in (38mm) nail through each dovetail to hold the corners together. Nail the backboard into place, and use it to hold the sides square with the top and bottom.

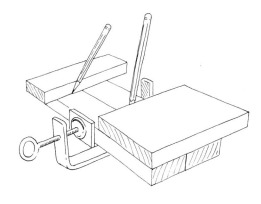

The doors

Saw out the doorframe members and smooth the sawn edges with a hand plane, then stack the pieces into two piles, one for each door.

Now cut the pieces to length, using a right-angle guide fitted to a circular saw. Clamp the sides together, and mark on the shoulder-lines for the top and bottom of the door. Then with the top and bottoms clamped, mark in the shoulders for the sides. Note that the shoulder-lines on the sides will be on the front faces, while the shoulder-lines on the top and bottom will be on the inside faces. Repeat on the other doorframe.

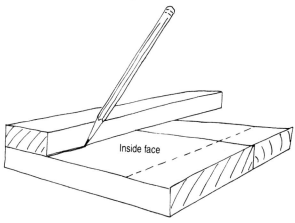

Inside face

Set the marking gauge to half the thickness of the doorframe, and mark all the joints. Shade the waste areas of each joint with a pencil, and check that you have got it right before cutting the shoulders.

These are long cross-halving joints, so before finishing with the saw, make several more cuts across the waste areas to weaken the waste wood, before chiselling it away as illustrated.

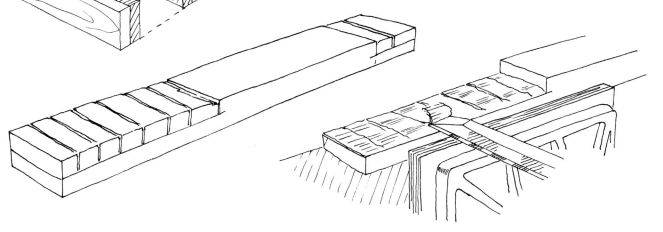

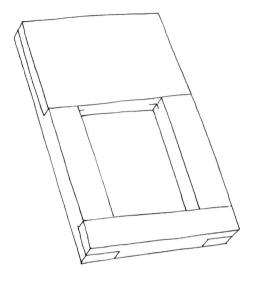

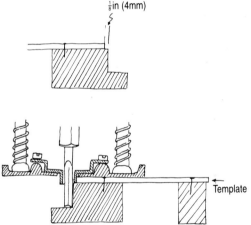

When all the cross-halving joints have been shaved almost to the gauge line, set the router in the router bench, lower the cutter to the exact gauge mark on the sides, and use the router to remove the last ¹⁄₁₆in (1.5mm) or so of waste (see page 35). Complete the work at each join by carefully chiselling away any waste remaining close to the shoulder-line.

Now glue and clamp together the four frame members of each door. Check that they are square before leaving them to dry.

Make a half-template of the arch. Pencil in the arches, and then cut them out using a jigsaw. Sandpaper the sawcut with 90 grit paper, backed by a curved block.

The glass rebate

Next cut out the rebate for the glass in the back of the door with a router. The easiest way to do this is to fit the template collar to the faceplate of the router, and make a template of the rebate. As both doors are the same, the template will be used twice. The diagram shows the relationships between the cutter, the template and the workpiece. The router cutter has to be a maximum of ¼in (6mm) diameter, in order to plunge through the collar. The outside diameter of the collar is ⅜in (9mm), so the edge of the template will have to be about ⅛in (4mm) further in from the side than the inside line of the rebate. Draw the template on a piece of ¼in (6mm) plywood or MDF, and cut it out with the jigsaw. Check the template by holding it over the door. The rebate line should be visible inside the template.

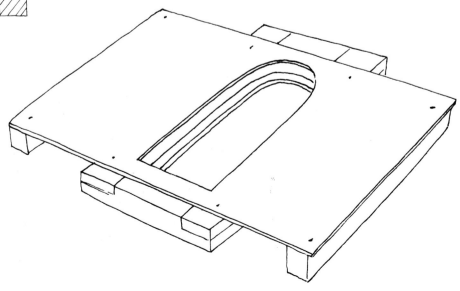

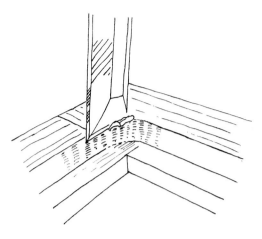

Nail the template to the inside face of the door and tack the overhanging ends of the template onto a pair of suitable blocks nailed to the bench. This arrangement holds the doorframe securely without marking its front face, and stabilizes the ends of the template.

Set the depth stop on the plunger to the depth you want, and work round the inside of the door until the rebate is finished. Swap doors and repeat on the second one. When both have been finished, use a sharp chisel to remove the radii at the corners of the doorframe.

Mouldings and pillars

The doors now have to be fitted with their applied mouldings. First, plane a length of timber 1½in (38mm) wide and ⅝in (15mm) thick. Use a circular saw to cut four 2in (50mm) lengths and four 1¾in (45mm) lengths from it. These are the top and bottom blocks, and you can sand their ends lightly to remove any roughness.

Take the rest of the 1½in (38mm) wide timber, and take a couple of shavings down its side, to reduce it by about ⅟₁₆in (1.5mm). Again using the circular saw, cut it into four lengths of 9⅝in (245mm) for the pillars. Each pillar is planed into the slightly curved shape illustrated. The apparent diameter at the top is slightly smaller than that at the base.

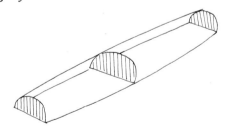

The easiest way to hold each pillar is to glue it temporarily onto the edge of a board, and clamp the board in the vice. You need to be able to run the plane down the edges of the pillar. An electric glue gun is an ideal tool for spot tacking: the bond is instant and does not spread far, so can be separated easily with a knife once the shaping is completed. If you do not have a glue gun, use thixotropic contact adhesive. Apply a blob of contact adhesive at each end of the pillar. Press the pillar in place to spread the glue to the holding board, and then separate the pieces for a few minutes until the glue is ready to make the bond.

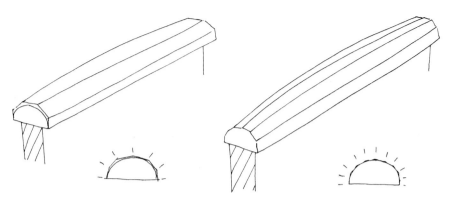

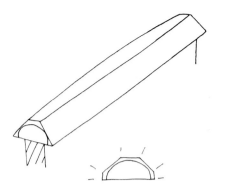

Plane the pillars in the sequence shown. Because you want a taper at the top of the pillar, you should start planing at the top, and then work towards the base. The first strokes of the plane remove the corners, the next widen the bevel, and the subsequent cuts meet in the centre of the pillar and reduce its thickness slightly. Now repeat the order, planing off the corners, until the pillar seems almost semicircular in section, apart from the small ridges running along it.

Sanding

Do not remove the pillar, but take some 90 grit sandpaper and back it with strips of masking tape. Now cut a strip of sandpaper about 3in (75mm) wide and pull it across the pillar vigorously. Move it along the pillar, taking care not to round off the very edges at the ends. Finish sanding the pillar with 150 grit paper, followed by 220 backed by a foam pad, and worked slightly across the grain. Repeat with the three other pillars.

Once the pillars are shaped and sanded, they can be rested on the doors. There is a gap of about ¼in (6mm) between the blocks and the pillars into which the bead is fitted. The bead is also shaped by hand, to match the section of the pillar.

Cut a strip of wood ¼in (6mm) thick and ⅝in (15mm) wide. Hold the end of the pillar over the strip as illustrated, and pencil round the curve of the pillar. Draw in a second curve ⅛in (4mm) outside the first one, so the bead will be slightly prominent. Cut off the section of strip that you have marked, and then use the chisel in a chopping motion to cut round the outer line you have just drawn.

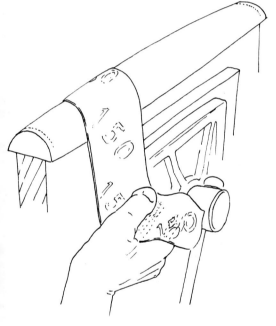

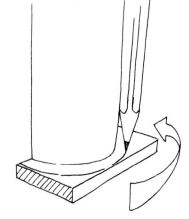

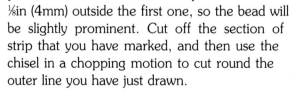

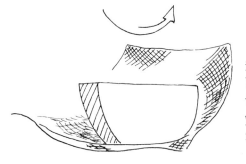

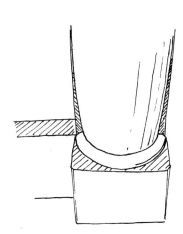

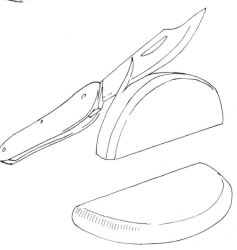

Sand the curve smooth by holding an offcut of 90 grit paper in the palm of your hand, and rubbing the bead strip into it. Use a penknife to cut a fine bevel on each edge of the curve, then round it again with the sandpaper cupped in the palm of your hand. Repeat for the other beads, and take care not to mix them up, they should be kept with the pillars they match.

Fitting and gluing

The applied decorations can be fitted as soon as the eight beads have been shaped. The easiest way to do this is to nail and glue them in position. Drive a couple of panel pins into the bottom corner of the door, and two more through the top corner, nailing through from the back. Hammer the panel pins through the cross-halving joints until their points just emerge on the front face of the door.

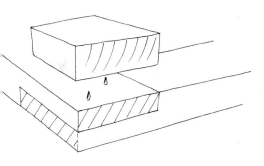

Position the bottom block at the corner of the door, and press it hard against the points of the nails. This will make an indentation in the block, which will help to locate it in position once the glue has been applied. Drive a couple more nails through the stile to anchor the pillar.

Repeat this nailing pattern on the opposite side of the door, and on the framework of the second door. Apply some glue to the inside face of the lower block and press it in position. It should locate easily on the two nail points poking through the corner. Turn the door over and hammer the nails into the block to hold it. Glue and fit the bead, then glue the pillar onto the doorframe. Press it down against the bead, and into the nail points.

Turn the door over and hammer the nails into the pillar, making sure that you have a smooth block on the bench to support the pillar when it is nailed. Now glue the bead and the top block, and nail these into position. Repeat on the other three stiles. Leave the doors lying face side up, and pile weights across the blocks and pillars to press them down while the glue dries.

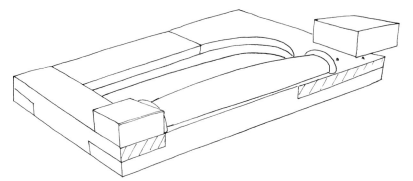

Fitting the shelves

The two shelves slide into the grooves cut on the inside face of the cupboard. Plane the shelves until they fit the grooves. Instructions for making the simple gallery of square-sectioned posts capped with a thin batten tacked on top can be found on page 66.

Fitting the doors

Each door is hinged on two 1½in (38mm) back flap hinges. The hinges should be set at the same height on both doors, and then screwed to the face of the doorframe as illustrated. It is important that the screws you use lie flush with the surface of the hinge. If the screws are prominent they will stop the hinge closing.

Now place the doors in position on the cupboard, make sure that they are aligned properly, and then use a knife to mark on the *edges* of the cupboard the precise location of the top and bottom of each hinge.

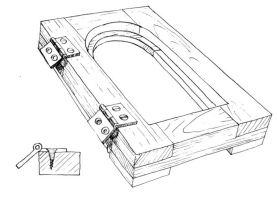

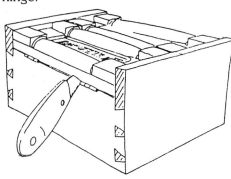

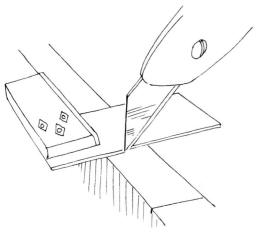

Remove the doors, and using a knife and set-square, square across the face of the cupboard side at each pencil mark. Set your marking gauge to slightly less than the full thickness of the hinge, and scribe a line on the side to connect the two lines. Repeat on the inside, and then do the same for the other three sets of marks.

Relieve the lines with a sharp chisel and then make the shallow sawcuts down the shoulder-lines as illustrated. Chisel out the waste between the sawcuts.

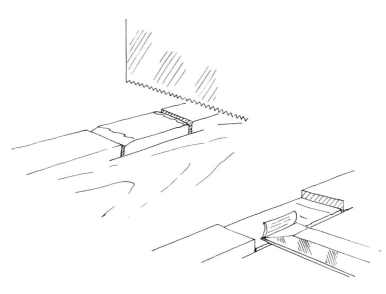

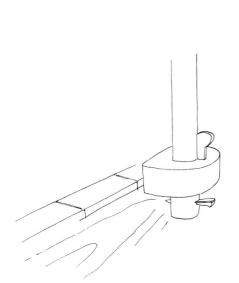

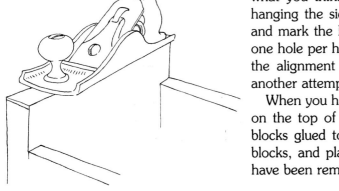

Now press the doors into place. If you have done everything accurately, the hinges will slip into the tight recesses carved for them, and stay there, so when you open the door it is easy to press a bradawl into the centre of each screw hole, and follow with a suitable screw. If they are a loose fit, hold each door in what you think is its correct position (with the hinges overhanging the side and edge of the door by identical amounts) and mark the hole centres with a pencil. Use the bradawl on one hole per hinge flap, and fit one screw. If you have not got the alignment quite right with the first screw you can have another attempt with the next screw (after removing the first).

When you have fitted the doors, close them. If the overhang on the top of the cupboard extends beyond the level of the blocks glued to the top of the door, mark the height of the blocks, and plane off the excessive overhang once the doors have been removed.

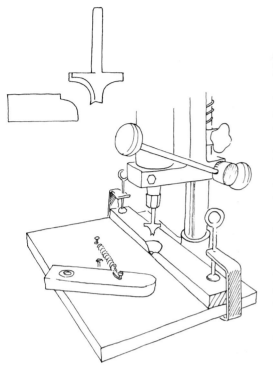

Fitting the base moulding

The base moulding is cut using a ⅜in (9mm) radius rounding over cutter set in the router. Choose a suitable straight-grained offcut of pine for the moulding. Set the router fence and the tool depth on the router bench, and cut a length of moulding sufficient for the front edge and returns at the side of the cupboard. You will probably have to make two passes across the cutter before you have a satisfactory moulding, lowering the tool to its full depth on the second pass.

Sand off the machine marks from the face of the moulding before sawing off the moulding from the edge of the board. Mark the mitres as illustrated, and saw them with a tenon saw. If you are a little unsure of your ability to cut these mitres by hand, make the simple mitre guide jig to help you cut them. Once the mitres to the front have been cut, glue and nail the front moulding in place. Then trim the mitres on the returns to meet the front, and glue them in place.

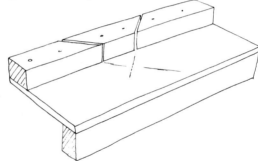

Punch the nail heads below the surface of the moulding and sand the mitres lightly to remove any unsightly roughness. Do not round off the corners, which should remain hard and clearly defined.

Making the cornice

It does not take long to make a short length of simple moulding, particularly if you can use a router to reduce the wood roughly to size before carving it with a gouge. Choose some straight-grained, knot-free pine or spruce for the cornice. The blank needs to be about 4in (100mm) longer than the width of the cupboard plus the two returns, which are equivalent to the depth of the cupboard. The extra length amounts to little more than the sum of the overhangs at the sides. Make a full-size template of a section of the moulding. Cut your blank to width and length, then draw the section onto each end.

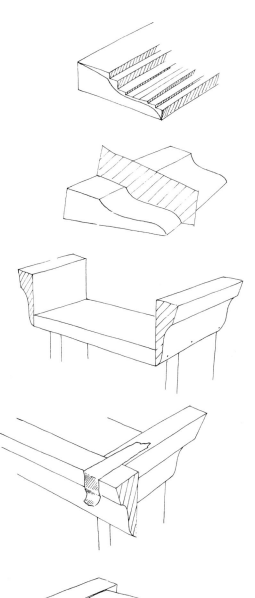

Now set up the router in the router bench, and fit it with a ⅜in (9mm) two-flute straight cutter. Set the fence and depth of the router bit with reference to the section of the cornice marked on its end, and remove most of the waste wood in a series of grooves running down the face of the blank.

Now screw the rough cornice moulding to a board, screwing through the board into the underside of the blank. Hold the board in the vice. There are some parts of the cornice that can be finished by plane. Smooth them carefully with the plane, and then take a gouge and carve the sweep of the cornice by hand. Finish chiselling one short length, before moving on. Check your work by holding the template against the cornice.

The moulding does not need to be very precise, because the joints at the corners are not mitres but simple butt joins which will easily accommodate minor variations in section.

When you have completed the handwork, select one or two blocks of a suitable section and use them as backing pads to support some 90 grit sandpaper. Smooth the face of the cornice, then change to 150 grit paper. Back it with a foam block, and using a slightly diagonal movement along and across the cornice, remove the rough sanding marks left by the coarse paper. Now change to a 220 grit paper, and adopting the same slightly diagonal motion, finish sanding it.

Then cut the two returns. Saw them on the electric saw-bench, using the right-angle guide, position them on the side of the cupboard as illustrated, and nail and glue them in place. Now glue the front of the cornice in position, holding it with pins along its lower edge, and with masking tape to bind its butt joints with the returns.

When the glue has dried, fit a couple of small, square glue blocks inside the corners, and using a tenon saw, chisel and gouge, change each corner into a gentle radius, following the steps illustrated.

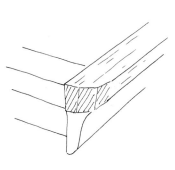
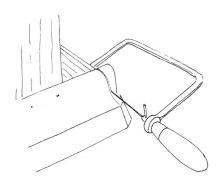

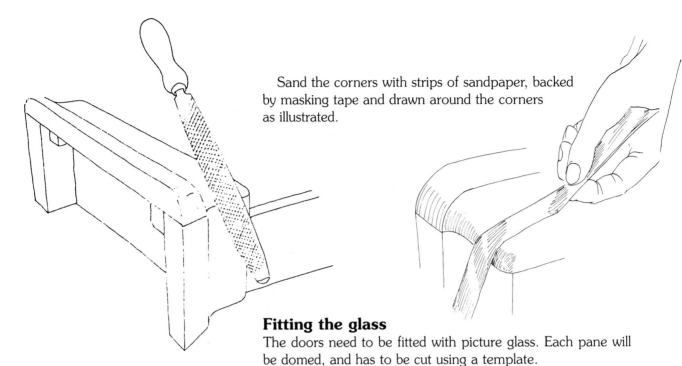

Sand the corners with strips of sandpaper, backed by masking tape and drawn around the corners as illustrated.

Fitting the glass

The doors need to be fitted with picture glass. Each pane will be domed, and has to be cut using a template.

Make a template of the inside rebate in the door, by holding a sheet of hardboard or thick card against the door, and pencilling around the edge of the rebate. You now have a record of the exact size of glass required, but most glass cutters would rather have a template they can cut around. It is worth telephoning your glazier to check, but usually the template they use is about ⅛in (4mm) inside the actual cut. (This is because the cutting tool itself is nearly ¼in (6mm) wide, and the cutter is set in its centre.)

Once you have checked what the offset should be, you can complete the template. It does not matter if it is a little inaccurate, as long as it is not too big, because there is plenty of room inside the rebate to conceal a loose fit.

When you have made the template choose some straight pine, and saw some narrow strips from its edge. These are to retain the glass. They should be fitted with mitres at the bottom of each door, and should stop at the start of the turn at the top of the door with a straight cut. Choose two (or perhaps a few more in case of breakages) particularly straight, clean strips for the ones that will be bent to fit inside the arch, and soak them overnight in a pan of water. Do not cut them to length yet.

The next day you should boil or at least leave them in very hot water for about 20 minutes, by which time they will be easy to bend into the required curve. Hold them in shape while they cool, and then trim them quickly to length with a chisel and slip them into the arch to set.

Fit the two shelves. A description for making the simple gallery is included on pages 65–6, where it is featured on the spice rack.

The glass is fitted after the cupboard has been stained, polished and waxed.

Staining and finishing

Dismantle the cupboard, removing the doors and shelves, and the thin strips that hold the glass. Fill the small number of nail holes in the cornice and base moulding with two-part filler, and then sand the cupboard with 220 grit paper.

Wipe a stain consisting of English Light Oak, American Walnut and Canadian Cedar (Colron stains), over the cupboard. Apply the stain quickly and thoroughly, in the direction of the grain. Avoid a heavy application of stain on the ends of the cornice, where there is a large area of exposed end-grain, and on the pillars, which are also likely to take in more stain than is desirable. If you find there is a problem with these areas, decant a little of the mixture, and add to it about 25 per cent (1–4) by volume of English Light Oak. Use this on the areas of end-grain, and work across towards these stains with the darker mixture afterwards.

Use a clean, dry rag to wipe away highlights on the pillars and cornice, and also on the doors above the arches.

Stain inside the doors, the shelves, and inside the cupboard, as well as inside and on top of the cornice. Leave the cupboard to dry for about 20 minutes, and then follow with a thinned brush coat of button polish.

You will need to apply about four coats of full strength button polish to this cupboard before rubbing down with 000 wire wool and waxing it with black wax. More detailed advice and a suitable finishing schedule for this cupboard can be found on pages 101–3.

Fitting the windows

Leave the shellac for a day or two to harden before fitting the windows. Place the door face down on some newspaper, and after cleaning the glass, place it in the rebate on the inside of the door. Slip the thin strips into the rebate, press them against the glass, and nail them into place with veneer pins. Snip off the pins once the points have penetrated the wood of the door by ¼in (6mm). Rehang the doors, this time holding each hinge with its full complement of screws.

LAKELAND
ARMCHAIR

THIS CRUDELY built chair is modelled on one I saw when visiting a large house near Penrith in Cumbria. The legs are chiselled to an octagonal section and wedged into the seat, which is cut out from a wide plank. The armrest is made from three solid planks, cross-halved together, and the sticks forming the back are chiselled and planed to a slight taper. You will not need a lathe to make this chair.

The example in the photograph (following page 96) is constructed from ash. The seat is slightly dished, which looks a lot nicer than a flat plank and is more comfortable. It was carved with a small hand adze. An alternative way of carving the seat is to sand it, using a hand-held angle grinder fitted with a cloth-bonded, flexible, abrasive disc.

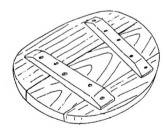

The chair seat illustrated is 2¼in (56mm) thick. If you cannot obtain wood as thick as this, make the seat from thinner planks, and support the underside with a couple of battens.

The legs are tapered towards the top, and splayed for stability. The holes for the chair legs are drilled right through the seat, and then chiselled to match the taper and section of the individual legs. The chair has been finished with stain and shellac.

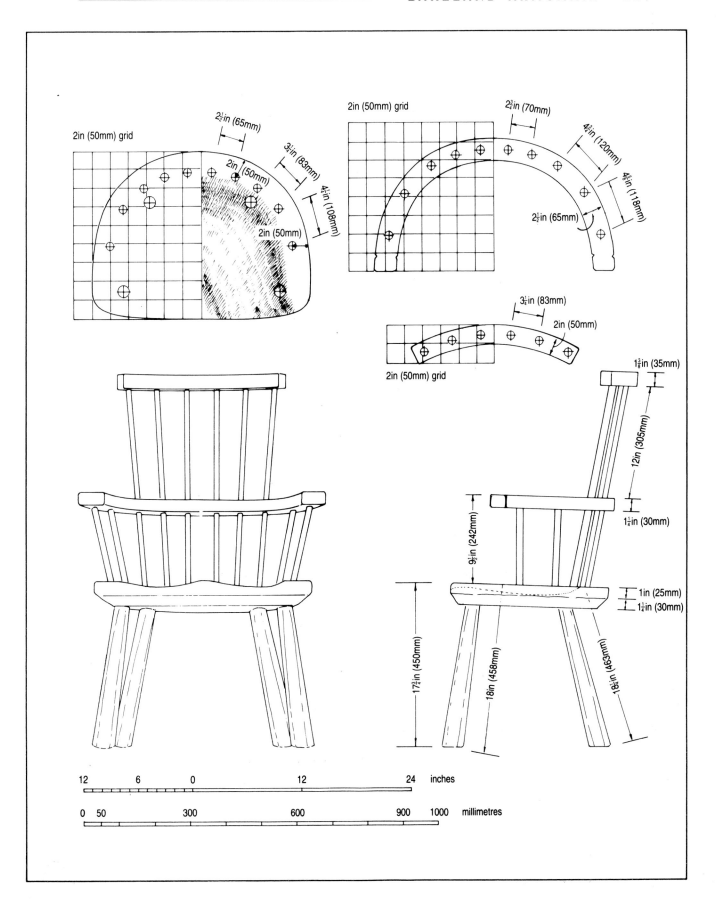

2in (50mm) grid

2½in (65mm)

3¼in (83mm)

2in (50mm)

4¼in (108mm)

2in (50mm)

2in (50mm) grid

2¾in (70mm)

4¾in (120mm)

4⅝in (118mm)

2½in (65mm)

3¼in (83mm)

2in (50mm)

2in (50mm) grid

1⅜in (35mm)

12in (305mm)

1¼in (30mm)

9½in (242mm)

1in (25mm)

1¼in (30mm)

17¾in (450mm)

18in (458mm)

18¼in (463mm)

12   6   0   12   24   inches

0   50   300   600   900   1000   millimetres

CONSTRUCTION

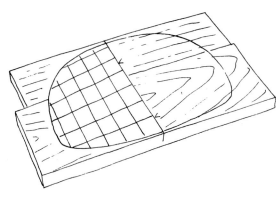

The seat

You will need a plank at least 1½in (38mm) thick for the seat. Ideally, the seat should be made from a single plank, but if you cannot find a piece of wood wide enough, you can join several narrow planks together.

Use the 2in (50mm) square grid on the plans to make a full-scale half-template of the chair seat. Lay the template on the plank you have chosen for the seat, and draw its outline.

Cut out the seat with a jigsaw equipped with a T101D blade, and hollow the seat with a hand adze, or with an electric angle grinder, to the sections shown in the illustration.

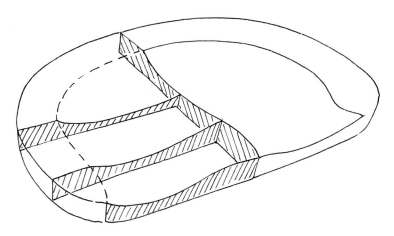

The illustration left shows how to hold the work while you are using the hand adze. It should be used with a steady swinging action, letting its momentum provide the energy to scoop out the timber. Make the cuts across the grain. Do not hack with an adze. There is plenty of weight in the tool to carry the blade through its cut, provided you use it accurately.

Try to remove a shaving with each drop of the adze. If the tool jams, your elbow is too low. If the tool hops upwards without making a cut, your arm is still too low.

Balance the work on its edge. At first you will find it difficult to control both the adze and the chair seat, but after a little practice you will learn to compensate with your right hand for wobbles in your left (or the other way round if you are left-handed). When you can do this, the work will proceed faster than it would if the seat were gripped in a vice, and there will be no danger of hitting the jaws of the vice with the adze.

For those using an angle grinder, fit the vacuum funnel to the side of the tool, and connect it to the vacuum cleaner. Clamp the seat to a trestle or bench, and remove the wood in channels, working towards the front. Make sure there is good ventilation and wear a breathing mask, as this is a dusty job.

When the seat is shaped, smooth it with an eccentric disc sander. This will remove the fish-eyes left by the angle grinder and the bumps and splinters left by the adze.

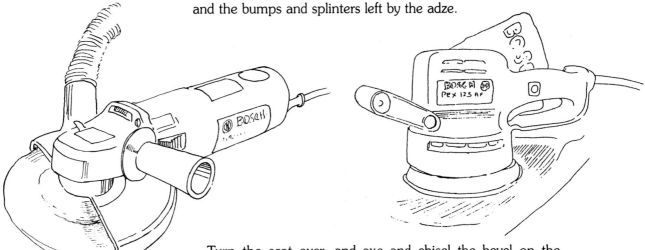

Turn the seat over, and axe and chisel the bevel on the underside of the seat as illustrated. If you think the seat needs some battens to strengthen it, fit them now. They should fit snugly, so it might be necessary to level the seat where the battens fit, using a chisel or an electric plane. Glue the battens to the seat and hold them with six short no.12 countersunk screws.

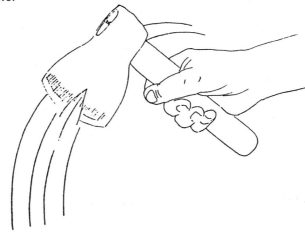

The legs

Cut out the four legs. These are made from wood 2½in (65mm) square. If you have a suitably straight-grained offcut from the end of a board, you can split the four legs from the plank with an axe, using a lump hammer to drive the axe-head into the edge of the plank. Whether or not the legs are shaped from machine-squared timber or roughly split from a board, the subsequent work should be careful and neat. This chair may be crudely constructed, but it is not poorly made.

Once the four legs are cut to length, trim them with a wide, sharp chisel to the slightly curved taper illustrated in the plans. As you work on the leg, try to keep its square-section constant. When all four legs are tapered to about 1½in (38mm) square at the top, chamfer the corners of the legs as illustrated opposite.

Fitting the legs

On the top face of the seat mark the four centrepoints for the leg holes. Each leg is splayed outwards, towards the corners of the seat. If the holes are drilled and then enlarged in stages, some adjustment can be made to the angle of the hole with each enlargement.

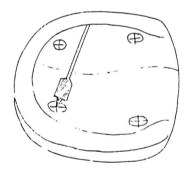 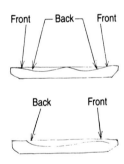

Drill the four holes from above the seat, and angle the drill bit outwards as you guide it into the seat. An assistant who can stand back and sight the angles for you would be a great help but, in the absence of any help, drill the four holes, and then poke a length of dowel into each one. This will give you a clear idea of how well you have done. Fit a larger diameter bit in the electric drill and, drilling from the underside of the seat, correct and enlarge the holes. Continue until all four holes have been drilled as well as possible, and each hole is about 1in (25mm) in diameter.

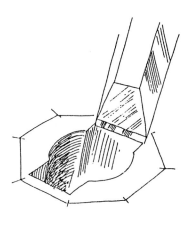

Now take one leg at a time and fit it into the underside of the seat. Mark the orientation of the leg, so that you can carve the tapered hole to fit the facets of the leg. Using a mallet and ⅝in (15mm) bevel-edged chisel, excavate the hole as illustrated.

As the leg penetrates deeper into the seat of the chair, the fit will become tighter, and the points where the leg jams will be more difficult to locate. Take some blackboard chalk, and rub it onto the sides of the chair leg. Press the leg in place, then tap it lightly with the mallet. Punch the leg out again, and chisel away the chalk marks in the hole in the seat. This is a slow, but accurate way of fitting the leg.

When all four legs are fitted, make a sawcut down the top of each one. Glue the end of the leg and tap it into the chair seat. Carve and slip a fine wedge into each sawcut, and hammer it in. Study the splay of the legs carefully, sight across the front and back legs and down the sides. The legs should spread evenly; if they do not, drive small wedges between the legs and the seat until they do. When the glue has dried, fill any remaining spaces with further small wedges.

Cut the legs to length (see page 130). Rather than leave a straight sawcut, chisel away the hard edges at the foot of the chair, until they are slightly rounded. Trim the top of the legs with a sharp gouge until they are flush with the seat.

The armrest

Mark on the perimeter of the seat the positions of the sticks which support the back and armrest.

The armrest is made from three solid planks of hardwood, cross-halved together, as illustrated below. Notice that a stick passes straight through each cross-halving joint for strength.

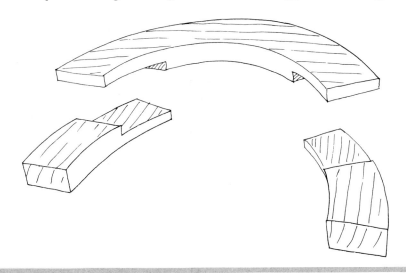

Using the grid marked on the plans, make two templates for the armrest: one for the centre back section, including the halving overlap, and one for the armrests, including the overlaps.

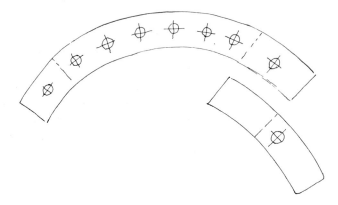

You will need a hardwood plank 8in (200mm) wide, 3ft 6in (1.07m) long and 1½in (38mm) thick for the armrest. Align the centre section template on the plank, and pencil round it. Cut it out with a jigsaw, then mark and cut out the two side sections. Make sure that the grain runs in the direction shown in the illustration. The short grain sections at the cross-halving joint are the weakest part of the armrest, so make sure that they are not weakened by fine cracks or splits.

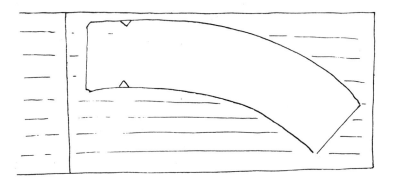

Mark and cut out the cross-halving joints at the ends of the centre section. Instructions for marking and cutting the joints are described on page 113. Trim the face of the joint to within about ⅟₁₆in (1.5mm) of the marking gauge line, and leave the accurate levelling for later when all the cross-halving joints can be trimmed with the router.

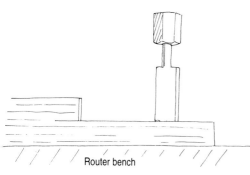

Router bench

Then mark and cut out the cross-halvings on the two end sections of the armrest in the same way, and trim them to thickness using the router fitted with a ⅜in (9mm) or ½in (12mm) straight two-flute cutter.

Gluing

Now glue the three sections of the armrest together. There should be no difficulty gluing them with hot animal glue, because the glue seizes the wood, and resists further movement. If you use PVA woodworker's white glue, there is a chance that when the cramps are applied the joint will slip. To prevent this, drive a couple of short pins into the ends of the jointing face as illustrated (keeping well clear of the areas which will be drilled for the back sticks).

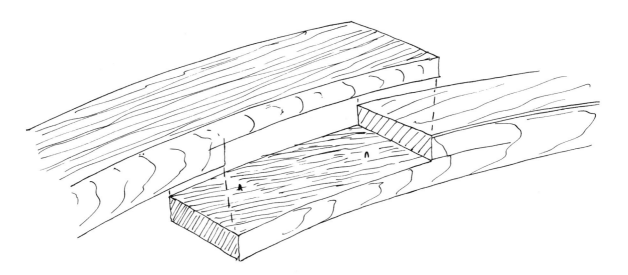

Snip off the heads of the pins, and press the joint together. The pressure will indent the jointing face and the pins will locate in the indentations, preventing movement when the cramps are applied.

When the glue has dried, plane and sand the outside of the armrest to a smooth and regular curve. Plane and sand the top and bottom faces of the armrests, then using the template again, or a pair of dividers reaching across from the outside curve, mark in the curve for the inside face. Trim that back with a chisel or spokeshave. Round the ends, and chisel a small radius on the corners of the backrest.

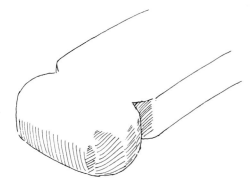

Backrest

Mark the location for each stick on the backrest. The longer sticks in the centre pass right through the armrest: the shorter pairs at the sides can pass right through to be trimmed flush, or the holes can be stopped short.

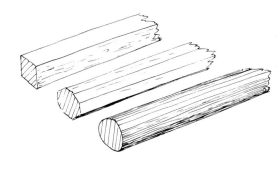

Cut all the sticks you will need from the edge of a straight-grained hardwood plank. Start with 1⅛in (28mm) square-sectioned battens, rough sawn, and plane off the corners. Remove the corners at the edge of each new facet, and work around the batten, trying to keep the number of plane strokes per corner the same. Once you have worked right around the stick, it should have a regular section. Repeat on the other sticks, then reset the plane to take a finer cut and work around each stick again, until it is reduced to a regular dowel, roughly ¾in (20mm) diameter, with only the finest flats visible on its surface.

When all the sticks are reduced to this approximate size, check the diameter of each one by boring a ¾in (20mm) hole in a scrap of wood then passing each stick through it. Trim down any sticks that are too fat to pass through the hole.

Sand each stick with 150 grit paper, backed by a foam pad. Sand in the direction of the grain. The slight ridges do not matter; the sticks do not need to look as though they have been turned.

ASSEMBLY

Now, using the ¾in (18mm) flat bit, bore the holes in the seat for the sticks. The holes should be stopped before breaking out of the underside of the chair, and should be drilled as well as you can to the angles illustrated in the plans. You should try to achieve the correct angles with the drill but, provided the centrepoints of each hole are regularly spaced around the perimeter of the chair, the precise angle at which they are drilled is not critical. Poke the sticks into the chair seat. You will find that with a little trimming and bending, they can be arranged to look right.

Using the template, mark the position for the holes in the armrest. You will need marks on both the top and underside of the armrest. The marks on the top should be central between the back and front faces of the armrest, while those on the underside should be marked slightly nearer to the front face, as illustrated.

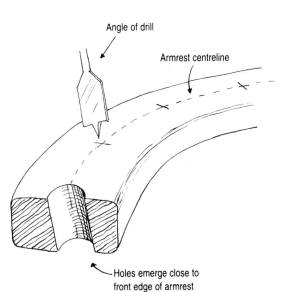

Angle of drill

Armrest centreline

Holes emerge close to front edge of armrest

Drill these holes with a fine drill, working first from the top. When you get halfway through the armrest, turn it over and drill the hole from underneath. If you do not want the short sticks at the side to poke through the armrest, you must stop the drill well short of the top surface. Later, when the holes have been enlarged to the correct diameter, you can gouge them deeper.

Fit the side sticks, tap them into position, adjust them until they line up correctly, mark their ends, and then cut them to length with a tenon saw. Bevel the top of the dowel with a penknife, check that the armrests fits solidly over the four sticks, then glue the assembly together. Now fit the longer sticks through the armrest into the seat, and glue them there.

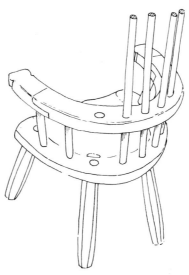

The comb is fitted last. Make a cardboard template for the comb, and cut it out of a 1½in (38mm) plank. It is almost square in section, and rounded at the corners. Drill the underside for the sticks in the same way as you drilled the ends of the armrest, so that the sticks do not break out of the top of the comb. Cut the sticks to length, bevel the edges of the sawcut and glue the comb into position.

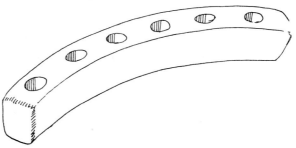

FINISHING

It is difficult to recommend a suitable finish for this chair, because it will depend upon the quality and the beauty of the woods that have been used in making it. If you have managed to collect together some particularly attractive woods, then a translucent stain, polished over with button polish (orange shellac) and waxed with black or brown wax would be fine. If parts of the chair, particularly the feet and the seat, are made from quite ordinary woods, then you might like to try to 'antique' the chair a little, adding some colour and tone to soften its appearance.

Translucent finish

Mix a quantity of English Light Oak and American Walnut stain together. Add a touch of Jacobean Dark Oak and test the colour on one of the upper parts of a leg. If you like the colour but decide it is not dark enough, try a second application. If this is still not dark enough, add a little more American Walnut and Jacobean Dark Oak. More than two applications of stain, one on top of the other will result in a blotchy finish.

When you are satisfied with the colour, wipe the stain over the seat and legs, then work up and down the sticks, comb and armrest. Do not bother to stain the underside of the seat.

Leave the stain to soak in for a few minutes then follow with a thin coat of button polish, thinned with methylated spirits and applied with a brush. Brush on three or four more coats of full-strength polish before leaving the shellac to harden for a few hours. Rub the chair down with 000 wire wool, and complete the finish with a generous application of brown or black, quick-drying wax.

Antique finish

Stain the chair as described above, and seal the stain with the thinned coat of shellac. Now stand back and assess the appearance of the chair. At this stage it can be disappointing, and perhaps look rather fresh and uninteresting. The base colour should be a warm, rich brown, and you can enhance this by toning down some parts of the chair to highlight other parts.

Lightly rub the chair all over with fine wire wool, and remove the dust. Now mix up some dry colours, Vandyke Brown, Brown Umber and Black, and add some PVA woodworker's white glue to the mixture. This will seem like a rough brown/grey paint, but it will colour the wood a deep brown.

Avoid adding any more red to the chair, as this will ruin the contrast of colours. Brush this mixture onto the back of the legs, the sides and top of the seat, and around its perimeter. Brush more along the outside edge of the armrest, and on the ends, back and top of the comb. Leave this paint to dry and then rub it lightly with wire wool.

The chair will now look a lot worse for your efforts. The paint will have gone grey and dull. When the dust from the wire wool has been vacuumed off, apply a second coat of thinned shellac polish to the uppermost part of the back chair leg. Hold this area to the light and look at it. The paint will now have turned from grey to deep brown. If it has gone black, take a rag and moisten it with warm water, wipe away the remaining paint from the seat and legs, and try mixing a fresh colour using less black. If the paint is the right colour, but a little too opaque, continue rubbing it lightly with wire wool, or dab at it with the damp rag to remove some of the colour. When you have found the right colour, apply several more coats of button polish to the chair, and leave it to dry.

It is still quite difficult to know how the chair will look when it is waxed. If you use black wax, the wax will tend to deaden the red tint in the stain, and whitish areas will seem slightly green. Brown wax warms all the colours up, but reduces the contrast between them. Aim to use black wax for this chair, and before applying it mix up an especially thick shellac to brush onto parts of the lower chair legs, the back of the comb and armrest and onto some of the back faces of the sticks. Take a cupful of shellac polish – garnet or button polish will do – and leave it out to evaporate for several hours. While it is thickening, mix up some aniline dyes in a methylated spirit solution. The colours you add should be predominently black and brown. Strain the mixture and add it to the shellac. Stir them together, then leave the shellac to thicken again.

Then take a 1in (25mm) brush and paint this mixture in the areas indicated in the illustration. Apply it quickly, and thickly, allowing it to run in one or two places. Wash the brush with methylated spirits.

Leave the chair for a while, and inspect it in a good light. You should now have achieved a quite convincing ageing effect. The 'original' finish will be visible in those areas not subject to wear, while the areas of the chair that are rubbed in use will be a warm brown. Add more of the paint and glue if you wish, and then rub the chair down with 0000 wire wool and wax it with black wax.

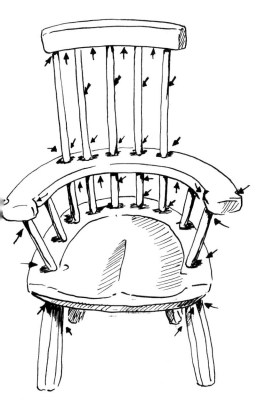

WORKSHOP
SKILLS

THE WORKSHOP

You do not need a large workshop to enjoy making furniture, but good lighting, an uncluttered floor and a good heater are essential.

Lighting is important. If possible place your workbench in front of a window, and arrange lights above and to one side of it. Double fluorescent tubes, or a powerful halogen light are ideal. Single fluorescent tubes flicker, and can be distracting and dangerous when you are using power tools.

If you have an electric planer or a circular saw bench, place them where they can cope with long pieces of timber.

Store stains and polishes in a steel cabinet. Shelves are useful, but get dusty; use cupboards for storing tools and jigs. Hang screwtop bottles full of nails, screws and pins beneath the wall cupboards by screwing their lids to the underside of the cupboards.

Hang the tools that you use most often on a board close to the bench. Put power tools on a shelf at shoulder height, and store the tools that you use only occasionally in a chest or box.

TOOLS

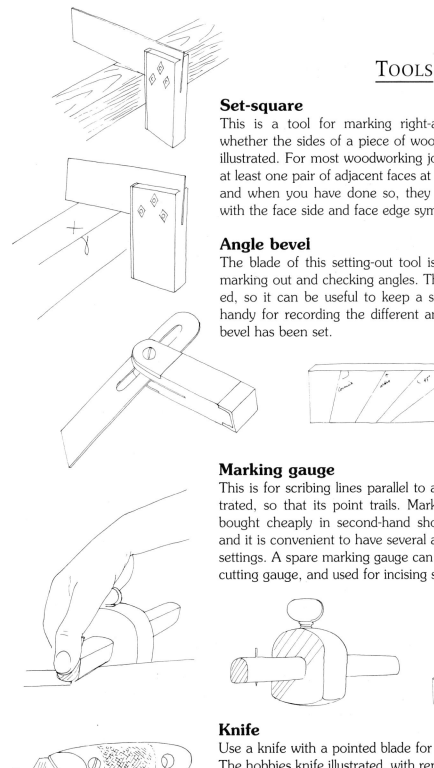

Set-square

This is a tool for marking right-angles, and for checking whether the sides of a piece of wood are square. It is used as illustrated. For most woodworking jobs you will need to plane at least one pair of adjacent faces at right-angles to each other, and when you have done so, they should be clearly marked with the face side and face edge symbols to avoid confusion.

Angle bevel

The blade of this setting-out tool is adjustable; it is used for marking out and checking angles. These tools are not calibrated, so it can be useful to keep a squared-up offcut of wood handy for recording the different angles at which your angle bevel has been set.

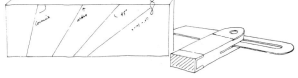

Marking gauge

This is for scribing lines parallel to an edge. It is held as illustrated, so that its point trails. Marking gauges can often be bought cheaply in second-hand shops and antique markets, and it is convenient to have several available at different useful settings. A spare marking gauge can easily be converted into a cutting gauge, and used for incising shoulder-lines and rebates.

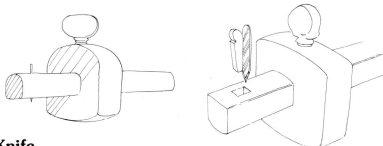

Knife

Use a knife with a pointed blade for marking out cutting lines. The hobbies knife illustrated, with replaceable and easily sharpened blades, is very useful.

SAWING

Tenon saw

This is a small saw used for accurate work. It will cut across and with the grain. It should be held in one hand as illustrated. It is quite difficult to make long or clean cuts across the grain with a tenon saw. Until the blade has a channel to work in, it tends to wander and abrade the surrounding wood. To avoid this, relieve the waste side of the line with a chisel, then hold the saw against the line and make a few tentative sawcuts. This slight step helps control the blade, and prevents it from tearing up the surface of the wood.

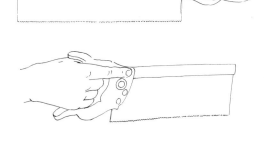

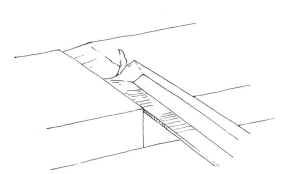

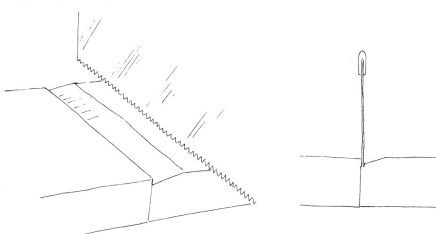

For cross-grain work use a home-made bench hook to hold the workpiece. You can use either end. One end lodges against the side of the bench, and the workpiece is pressed against the other. Make a simple mitre block to assist with sawcuts of 45°.

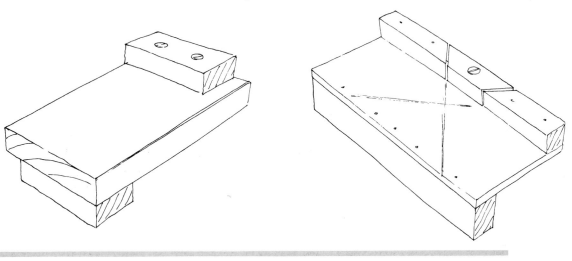

Handsaw

The handsaw is used for making quick and accurate sawcuts through large pieces of wood. It is held as illustrated, with the first finger pressed against the side of the handle. Support the work on a trestle or in a vice. Do not press the saw into the wood, or it is likely to wander off course.

When you are cutting the cheeks of a tenon, hold the wood in the vice and start the saw on the waste side of the line, guiding the blade with your thumb.

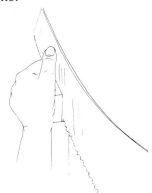

Tilt the saw at first, but when the sawcut is sufficiently established to guide the blade, you can raise the handle and bring the blade level.

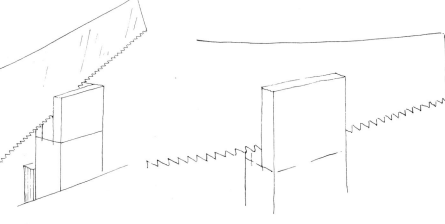

Coping saw

The blade has coarse, quick-cutting teeth, which make this an ideal tool for removing waste from between dovetail pins etc. The blade is tensioned by the sprung sawframe, and can be swivelled to enable the saw to cut complex shapes close to the edge of a board.

Circular saw

The circular saw illustrated has a large table and additional supports to hold the work. It has a parallel fence and a sliding adjustable fence which feeds work into the blade. The height of the blade above the table can be adjusted by a wing nut under the table. Arrange good lighting, and wear safety glasses and ear muffs. Use notched sticks to push and control the work, and never, not even when you are in a hurry, allow your hands close to the blade, either to feed the work or to remove it.

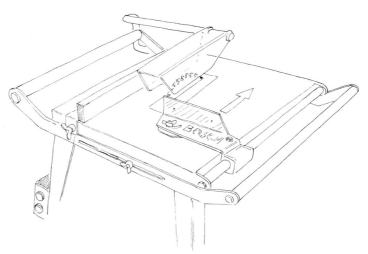

Jigsaw

The jigsaw is a powerful and versatile saw. The example illustrated will cut wood up to 3in (75mm) thick, in straight lines and in curves. Choose a jigsaw which has an orbital cutting action. When the orbital action is engaged, the blade draws itself into the wood and requires less forward pressure.

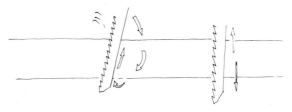

Disengage the orbital action when you are cutting tight curves or approaching another sawcut. Keep both hands well clear of the blade. The right hand controls the variable speed trigger, and the left tucks behind the tool, controls its direction, and applies a little forward pressure. Always ensure that the electrical lead is kept behind and clear of the blade.

PLANING

Planes

You will need a shoulder or block plane, and a smoothing plane.

The shoulder plane is versatile: it can plane across the grain, smooth end-grain and plane with the grain. It is small enough to fit into the palm of the hand and, because it is light and copes with the most turbulent grain, I find I use it more than any other plane. The blade is set at a low angle, with the sharpening bevel on the top face of the blade as illustrated.

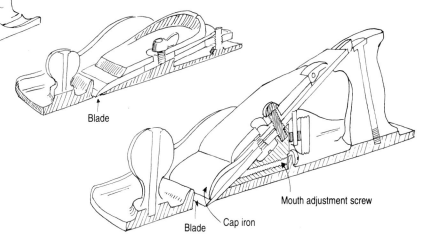

Blade

Mouth adjustment screw

Blade   Cap iron

The smoothing plane is larger, and its blade is set at a steeper angle. It is a big, powerful plane, used with both hands. It will remove wood quickly, and leave a smooth and satisfactory finish. Instructions for sharpening plane blades can be found on pages 150–52.

Planing wood by hand is energetic work. Try to work in the best possible conditions. Make sure that the wood is well supported, and clamped if necessary. Rub candle wax on the sole of the plane to lubricate it, and strop or sharpen the blade regularly (see page 152). The width of the mouth of both these planes can often be adjusted; a narrower mouth is usually set when making particularly fine shavings. After adjustment, always ensure that the screws and locking screws are tightened securely, otherwise the plane will chatter.

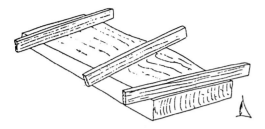

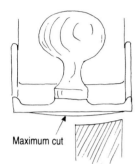

Maximum cut

Squaring a piece of wood

For making the furniture illustrated and described in this book, you will need to be able to plane two adjacent sides square with each other. First, check the timber for twists. Sometimes a twist is quite obvious, but by placing sticks across the timber, as illustrated, it is possible to sight the board accurately, identify the high spots and plane them flat. When you have removed the twist on one face, mark it with the face side mark (see page 139), then try to find an adjacent side which is at right-angles to it. Check the angles with a set-square.

Take one of your two hand planes. If you sight down the blade, you will find that there is a slight curve to the blade's edge. The blade will cut more wood with the centre of the blade than at the sides. To plane the edge square, all you have to do is position the plane on the edge and adjust the lateral position of the plane as you push it forward, as illustrated. Control the position of the plane with the left hand, pressing the fingers against the side of the timber to align the plane on the edge as required.

Trailing fingers

Trailing fingers give
lateral control

Planing end-grain

Planing end-grain is hard work, and it is always worthwhile sharpening or stropping the blade to help reduce the amount of effort required. The problem when planing across the end of a piece of wood is that edges of the board are likely to split. To avoid this, you should try to plane the end-grain before trimming the sides, so that the marred wood can be removed.

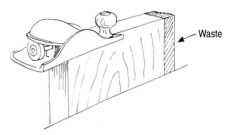

Waste

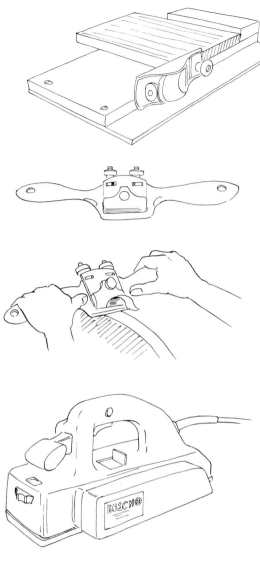

If you want to plane the end-grain without damaging the sides, adopt some of the measures illustrated, or use a shooting board.

Spokeshave

The spokeshave is held with two hands, and drawn towards you. The depth of cut is controlled by the knurled screws which hold the blade. When you are adjusting the blade, or after sharpening it, withdraw the blade with the two screws, and then gradually wind them in, keeping the blade in contact with the screws. Tighten the clamping iron against the blade to help hold it in position.

Electric planer

This is a very useful tool if you are using rough-sawn timber for your furniture. The depth of cut is adjusted by the wheel at the front of the plane. A depth stop can be clamped to one side of the plane, and a parallel fence for squaring up timber to the other. Whenever you can, you should fit the vacuum hose attachment to the planer. This is fitted instead of the shavings bag and, although the plane is more cumbersome when connected to the tube, it can be used continuously.

Wear ear muffs and safety glasses when you are using an electric planer. Clamp the wood firmly. Apply downward pressure on the front handle as you feed the plane onto the wood, and firm pressure on the back handle as the plane leaves the timber. This will prevent the revolving cutting irons from scooping out a transverse groove on its entry and exit from the wood.

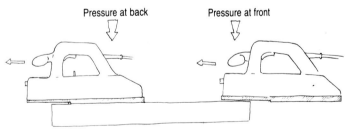

Pressure at back   Pressure at front

If you are planing a large plank, you must first plane off the highspots and eliminate any twist. Three winding sticks used across the board (see page 144) will identify areas that need to be shaved down. When the surface is level, you can plane its surface in regular, straight strips. The thicknessing device illustrated enables stock up to 3in (75mm) wide to be thicknessed and squared up.

Chisels

You will need 1½in, ⅝in, ½in, ⅜in and ¼in (38mm, 15mm, 12mm, 9mm and 6mm) chisels. The largest is a firmer chisel with a strong, square-sectioned blade. The others are much more delicate, and are known as bevel-edged chisels.

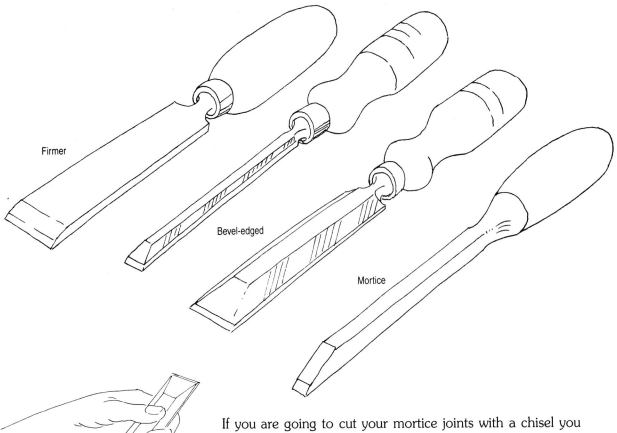

Firmer

Bevel-edged

Mortice

If you are going to cut your mortice joints with a chisel you should buy strong, thick-bladed mortice chisels, which have a shock absorber in the handle. For most work, the chisels are held as illustrated. One hand controls and guides the cut, while the other applies the forward pressure. Always keep your hands behind the line of the cut.

Chisels must be kept extremely sharp. The sharper they are, the easier they are to use, and the safer they are. Instructions for sharpening chisels are given on pages 150–52. If you want to apply a sustained heavy pressure on the chisel, lodge your right elbow against your hip or, if you are chopping downwards, brace your shoulder against your right hand and use your body weight to supply the extra power.

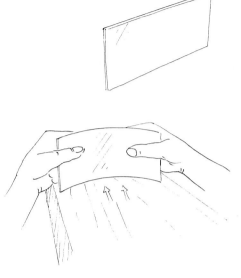

Cabinet scraper

A cabinet scraper is a straight-sided, thin plate of hard steel. It is held as illustrated, and drawn or pushed along the grain of a piece of wood to smooth it. It works best on hard, dense woods. A fine hook is worked on both edges of each side. This removes a fine shaving as it is drawn across the timber.

To sharpen a cabinet scraper, grind off any traces of a previous burr with an oilstone. Clamp it in the vice, as illustrated, then take a fine, flat file and, holding it on the edge of the scraper, remove the used edge. File carefully until the new edge is flat and hard-edged. Now, take the back of a gouge or shank of a screwdriver as a burnishing iron, and draw it once or twice along the edge. Follow with a couple of light strokes along each side to form the hook. After a little use, the scraper will lose its edge, and you can then turn it around and use a new corner.

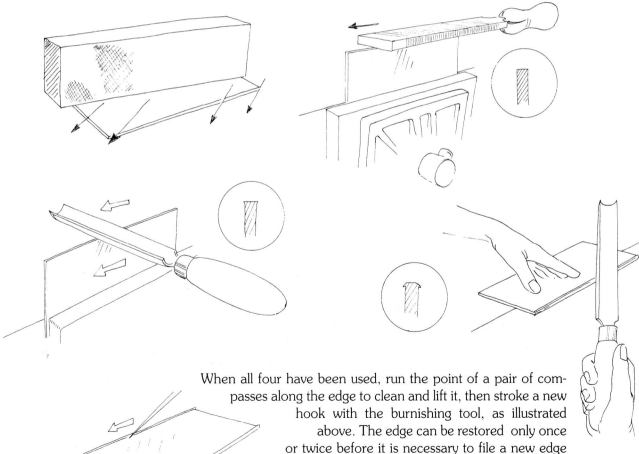

When all four have been used, run the point of a pair of compasses along the edge to clean and lift it, then stroke a new hook with the burnishing tool, as illustrated above. The edge can be restored only once or twice before it is necessary to file a new edge and form new hooks.

SANDING

You will need several grades of abrasive paper: 60, 90, 150, 220 and 440. The numbers refer to the size of the abrasive particles. Metal sandplates are particularly useful, last a long time, and are easy and comfortable to use. When you are sanding, start with fresh 90 grit paper, back it with a foam or cork block and, without pressing hard, sand diagonally down the grain. Smooth the surface and remove the blemishes with this rough paper, then change to 150 grit, and alter the angle slightly, so that you are sanding almost parallel with the grain. Continue with the 150 grit paper, and remove all the marks left by the 90 grit paper. Change the paper again to 220 grit, and sandpaper parallel with the grain. Finish with 440 grit paper. The same system of changing to finer grit papers applies when you are using the power sanders illustrated below.

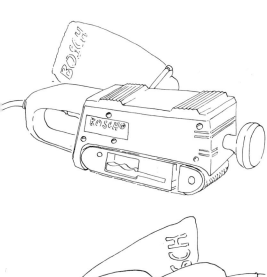

The belt sander

This is an invaluable tool which will smooth a large, rough surface quickly and easily. Change the belts regularly and do not press hard. A bench mounting clamp enables you to sand small pieces.

The eccentric disc sander

This is another powerful and versatile tool. The easily changed sanding discs are available in a variety of grades, and hold themselves to the rotating head with a Velcro-like grip. The eccentric rotation pattern of the head means that stock is removed rapidly, without leaving concentric scratches on the wood. Its compact size makes it an ideal tool for smoothing the seat, legs and armrests of the Lakeland armchair.

Orbital sander

When you are using an orbital sander, you must either wear a breathing mask or connect your sander to a vacuum cleaner. You should not inhale the very fine dust that orbital sanders generate. Change the paper frequently, and inspect its surface regularly. Sometimes small pieces of grit become trapped, tearing the paper and scoring the work.

Disc sander

Fit a rubber backing pad to this powerful tool, and use cloth-bonded abrasive discs. Hold it with both hands, connect the vacuum attachment, and use the edge of the disc to shape the scooped seat of the Lakeland chair.

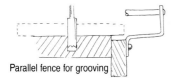

Parallel fence for grooving

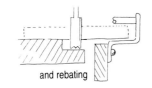

and rebating

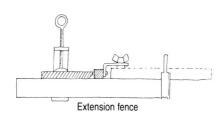

Extension fence

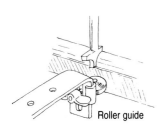

Roller guide

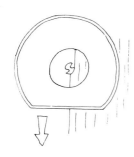

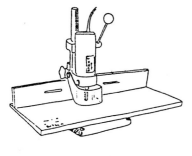

ROUTER

This is probably the most versatile power tool available to the home woodworker. The router illustrated is fitted with a ¼in (6mm) collet for holding the cutters.

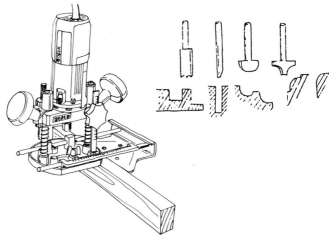

The accessories include two fences, a template and roller guides. A range of cutters is shown. The profile they cut varies according to the depth to which the tool is plunged. When you change cutters, it is important to make sure there is sufficient shank held in the collet before you tighten up the clamping nut. Tighten all the other nuts and bolts on the router before it is used, or they will shake loose.

When you are using the router as a hand-held tool, pull the router against the rotation of the cutter, as illustrated. If you use it the other way, it leaves an unsatisfactory finish, and is difficult to control. When working without a fence, use a minimum depth setting. Scorching is caused either by a blunt cutter, or a feed rate that is too fast. Sometimes the waste in a groove or mortice is trapped, and scorching results. Where there is a likelihood that the cutter will overheat (for example when you are grooving or morticing), plunge the router in short steps, and clear the groove with shallow cuts. Buy carbide-tipped straight cutters.

The router can be mounted in a bench stand. Fences can be clamped, tacked or bolted to the surface of the bench. The depth stop controls the depth of cut, and the long lever raises and lowers the cutter and motor.

When you are using a router, always wear safety glasses and ear mufflers.

SHARPENING

All woodworking edge tools need to be kept sharp. Sharpen tools before they become dull and hard to use. Once a cutting edge begins to break down, it rapidly deteriorates, and the longer the delay in resharpening the greater will be the task when it is undertaken. Be alert for indications that the blade is dulling. Sharp edge tools make a faint singing sound as they slice through fibres of wood. A dull tool digs away, the efforts of the worker adding to the sound of chatter and the splitting of wood fibres. A simple test is to hold the edge of the blade to the light. A sharp blade will not reflect light from its cutting edge. A dull blade can quickly be identified, as the chipped or slightly blunted parts glitter.

A sharp blade cuts cleanly and evenly. Minor variations in the grain will not cause the tool to hesitate or stick. The balance of effort between pushing, guiding and restraining the tool will be easy to maintain.

The illustration shows suitable sharpening angles for a chisel or plane iron used for cutting softwood and hardwood. The angles are slightly different, and are meant as a guide.

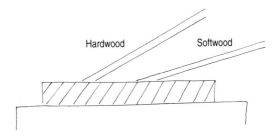

Equipment

You will need a grindstone, a medium and a fine oilstone, and some stropping compound.

Grinding the tools

You do not need to use the grindstone very often, but every now and again, when you inspect the edge of a troublesome tool, you will notice that, despite your best efforts at honing, the sharpening angle has become rather steep. If you compare it with the angle illustrated here, you will realize that grinding the tool back to its correct angle by hand will take a long time, and be hard work.

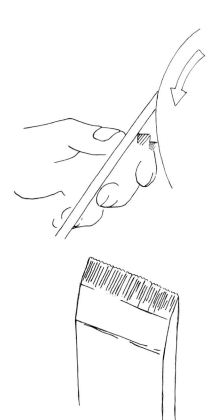

Electric grindstone

Once you have decided to use the grindstone, check your other edge tools, and sharpen those that need attention at the same time. Switch on the grindstone, and hold the tool against the stone, as illustrated. Move it sideways to left and to right, easing the pressure on the tool as you reach the edges. If you hold the tool against the grindstone for too long, it will over-heat, so when you have made two or three passes over the stone, swap tools and grind the next. When the sparks flying off the grindwheel begin to pour down the back of the blade it is time to stop. Inspect the blade: the grindstone should have raised a ragged burr at the edge, as illustrated.

Oilstone

Now drip a few drops of oil onto the oilstone, and grind away the burr. Hold the tool as illustrated and try to maintain a constant angle between the tool and the oilstone. After five firm strokes along the face of the oilstone, turn the blade over and remove the burr with a single flat stroke. Repeat several times, each time reducing your hand pressure.

Lubricate the smooth oilstone, and repeat the procedure, keeping the tool at a constant angle. When you hone the bevel, you are raising the burr at the edge, and when you turn the tool over and hone its back flat against the stone you are removing the burr. Try to keep the proportion of strokes 5:1, five strokes on the bevel to each flatting stroke on the back. Reduce your hand pressure with each group of strokes.

As you look at the trail left on the surface of the oilstone, you will notice that the trails left by the ragged burr are slowly eliminated.

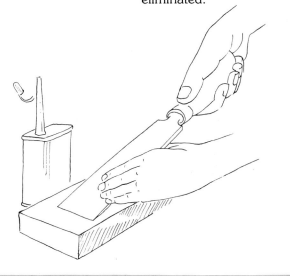

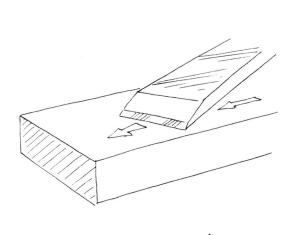

Strop

Make a strop by rubbing stropping compound onto a leather strap. Keep one side for the coarse compound, and the other for the fine. Repeat the honing procedure on the strops, first on the coarse, then on the fine: five strokes on the bevel to each stroke on its back. Lines left on the surface of the strop will indicate that there are still notches in the edge of the blade. If the tool is old and slightly pitted, it may be impossible to improve on what you have done, but if the tool is not rusty, you should go back to the oilstone and try once more to remove the awkward nick.

When you are happy with the edge of the tool, use it to make a vertical slice across some end-grain. The blade should slice through the corner with little effort, and leave a clean, unscored face. Alternatively, you can hold a sliver of paper in one hand, and try to cut down its unsupported edge with the blade. A sharp blade will make a clean cut.

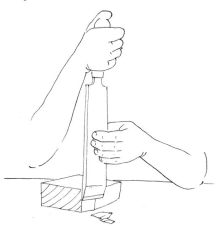

Keeping tools sharp

Once you have sharpened your tools, try to keep them sharp. Strop them frequently while you are using them, and store them carefully. When you are planing, lift the plane on its return stroke, and when you put the plane down, place it on its side. Store your chisels in a tool roll or in racks, where they cannot knock against each other. When you are sharpening lathe tools, the skew chisels and the parting tool are ground and stropped as described above. Gouges and scrapers need only to be ground against a rough grindstone, and used still with their ragged edge. Grind these latter tools to 45° or slightly more, to give a strong, heat-absorbing edge.

WOODS

A notable feature of many pieces of country furniture is that they are often made from a variety of different woods. Usually, the best quality woods, such as oak, yew or cherry are given prominence, and poorer quality offcuts of pine, poplar or chestnut are used for the sides and backs. These inferior boards are often split and warped. Sometimes they still show sapwood and bark, and are often very knotty.

In addition to this, the planks are frequently thicker than necessary, and where they cannot be seen are left rough. The outside back of a country armoire, or cupboard, will often be left rough-sawn, or adzed.

For anyone wanting to make their own furniture, this country tradition of making do and using what is available, is rather a blessing, particularly for those who have a collection of really useful pieces of wood. It is also an opportunity to use knotty and warped timbers that are often strikingly beautiful. They are more trouble to work, because the joints have to be planned carefully to avoid weaknesses, and their turbulent grain makes them difficult to smooth, but they will repay the trouble they cause.

In time the panels, frames and moulding will warp, and your home-made cupboard will become an authentic example of country furniture.

Woodyards

The easiest way to obtain wood is to visit your local DIY super-store, where you will find abundant quantities of white wood. If you enjoy the appearance of these woods, this will be a convenient source of supply; the timber will be dry, shrink-wrapped, planed on all four sides and ready for immediate use. If it is bought in this state, you will not need to have planers, sanders, or even a circular saw. Construction will be straightforward, and results satisfactory.

The alternative suppliers are builders' merchants and timberyards. Visits to these places will involve time and trouble, but it will be worth it. The wood may not cost less, but it may well be better quality. There will be an enormous range to choose from and you will learn about the woods from the people who serve you. Although it is difficult to select wood, it is fun to try, and exciting to discover the wealth of potential stored in the yard.

Visiting a woodyard

Before you enter a woodyard you should have a clear idea of what wood you need. You should list the wood sections that you want, and then calculate the lengths. If you are visiting a small, privately run yard, it is unlikely that you will find many planks more than 6 or 7ft long (1.83–2.13m); so there will be little point in specifying one plank 12ft (3.66m) long, when what you really need is one 5ft (1.52m) plank and one 7ft (2.13m) plank.

Make a list which specifies the component, the number of identical components, the thickness, width and length. Leave room on the list against each component for a plank number, so that you can number off the planks with chalk once you have decided how you will use them.

ITEM	No. OFF.	SECTION	LENGTH	TOTAL LENGTH	PLANK No	COMMENTS.

Most timberyards store their wood outside in stacks. Usually a stack will be composed of a single trunk that has been sawn through and through. By inspecting the ends of the planks and their position in the pile, you will know from which piece of the trunk it was cut. By inspecting the side (which will often be covered in bark) you should be able to gain some idea of the quality of the board. If the bark is smooth and straight, you should expect a straight-grained board with few blemishes. If the board has an evenly rippled edge, it may well have an iridescent figure. If you see places where limbs have been sawn off, you should expect a troubled (but often attractive) grain pattern.

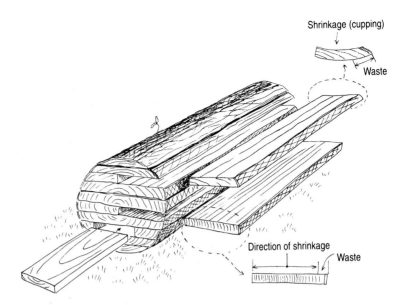

Shrinkage (cupping)

Waste

Direction of shrinkage

Waste

You must inspect each piece. Negotiate the price down if the wood is split, knotty, or discoloured. Do not buy it if it is already twisted, or has a soft, furry surface. Such wood will misbehave from the moment you try to tie it on the roof rack. The section through the tree trunk illustrated should give you some indication of the qualities you can expect from boards sawn from it.

Storing wood

When you have bought your wood from the woodyard, cut it roughly to size, and stack it in a warm place to dry. Rest each piece on a row of thin wooden battens, to allow air to circulate through the stack. Freshly cut timber stored outside takes about a year to dry out for every inch of thickness. After this time the wood can be used, but it is worthwhile taking the wood you plan to use into your house to dry out for a week or two before you need it.

GLUES

You should equip your workshop with a variety of glues. The glues you will use most are woodworking glues, but you will also find that it is useful to have a tube of instant drying superglue and a tube of thixotropic contact adhesive. You might not use them in the joints of the furniture, but you may well find them useful in making jigs, and for temporary clamping.

PVA glue

This is a versatile glue. It is easy to apply, can be thinned with water for making paints, and it dries clear. In addition, it has the advantage of being slightly flexible, so joints made with this glue can accommodate a certain amount of shrinkage.

PVA glue is slippery, which sometimes makes lining up and clamping a joint tricky. It is often necessary to roughen a surface or drive in short tacks to reduce the risk of two pieces sliding out of alignment as they are glued together.

The high water content means wood coated with PVA tends to swell. This can make it difficult to drive in a dowel or to press a tenon into a tight mortice, particularly if you leave the pieces to stand once they have been smeared with glue. If you are assembling a tight-fitting set of joints, practise the assembly procedure, then apply the glue and work quickly.

PVA glue dries to a transparent film, and although it cannot easily be seen when the furniture is unstained, the film of glue will mask the wood and spoil the staining. When using PVA wipe off excess glue with a wet brush or rag before it has a chance to dry.

Animal glue

This is the traditional woodworker's glue. It is applied hot, and grabs the wood as it cools. It shrinks as it dries, pulling joints together. It is gap filling and strong. Animal glue is not waterproof and, like wood, is subject to variations in humidity. Because of this, it allows movement between planks due to shrinkage or swelling.

Try to use fresh glue; glue that has been reheated loses its strength. Prepare the glue the night before you need it. Cover the pearls with cold water and leave the container to stand. The pearls will swell, ready for use in the morning. Heat the glue in a double boiler or in a saucepan, over a low heat. The water can boil, but you should avoid boiling the glue. Keep the glue

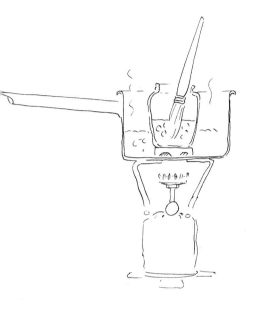

brush in the water surrounding the glue tub. After some use, this water will have its own glue content, and can be used for sizing a joint, prior to gluing.

Work in a warm room. If you have large pieces of wood to glue together, warm the gluing faces in front of a heater before applying the glue, to prevent it being chilled by the cold wood. When you are ready to apply the glue, dip the brush into the pot. The glue should run like thin syrup from the tip of the brush. If necessary, add hot water to dilute the glue and stir it.

Brush the glue onto the joint, and press the pieces together. If you are making a long butt joint, rub the pieces together, and leave them with their ends and edges aligned. If the joints have been accurately planed, they will not need to be clamped. Wash off surplus glue with a clean brush and hot water, and wipe them dry with a rag.

Sizing a joint

Some woodworkers prefer to size a joint before gluing it. This involves brushing dilute glue onto the gluing faces, rubbing them clean with a cloth, then following with the full strength glue. This seems to give a stronger joint, and is often done when thin panels are glued together.

Cascamite

This is an extremely strong, waterproof urea-formaldehyde glue, simple to mix and easy to apply. Cascamite is bought in powder form. To mix it you add a small quantity of water to a portion of powder and stir to a thick paste.

Setting times depend on temperature; the mixed glue remains usable for approximately 3 hours at 15°C (60°F), giving ample time for making adjustments when a joint is being clamped together. It is a satisfactory gap-filling glue. Wash off excess glue from the work and rub it dry. Rinse your hands after handling Cascamite because contact with the skin can cause dermatitis.

Cascamite dries hard and brittle. Mix the glue in the bottom half of a washing-up liquid bottle. These are made from a flexible plastic, so once the glue has gone hard it is easy to remove the hardened residue and re-use the container.

SUPPLIERS

Most of the materials and tools required to make the pieces of furniture featured in this book can be obtained from your local hardware store, but I include a short list of specialist companies which you might find useful. They have a thorough knowledge of their speciality, and are always able to give useful advice. Their service is prompt and reasonably priced.

Wood
Interesting Timbers, Church Farm, Easton Grey, Malmesbury, Wiltshire SN16 0PS

Cabinet-Makers' Finishing Materials
Fiddes and Son Ltd, Florence Works, Brindley Road, Cardiff CF1 71X

Brassware
John Lawrence and Co. (Dover) Ltd, Granville Street, Dover, Kent CT16 2LF

Tools
Sarjents Tools, 44–52 Oxford Road, Reading, Berkshire RG1 7LH

The following American companies have been recommended to me:

Wood
Maurice L. Condon Co. Inc., 248 Ferris Avenue, White Plains, NY 10603

Tools and Brassware
Woodcraft, 41 Atlantic Avenue, PO Box 4000, Woburn, MA 01888

INDEX